CROHAM HURST SCHOOL
1899-1999
Time Present and Time Past

Croham Hurst School in Miss Clark's day.

CROHAM HURST SCHOOL
1899-1999
Time Present and Time Past

Monica Sharpe

Phillimore

1999

Published by
PHILLIMORE & CO. LTD.
Shopwyke Manor Barn, Chichester, West Sussex

Croham Hurst School
79 Croham Road
South Croydon
Surrey   CR2 7YN
Telephone: 0181 680 3064   Fax: 0181 688 1142
e-mail: admin@Croham_hurst_school.dialnet.com

ISBN 1 86077 084 3

Printed and bound in Great Britain by
BOOKCRAFT LTD.
Midsomer Norton

CONTENTS

LIST OF ILLUSTRATIONS

FOREWORD

It has been a common aspiration for many years that a history of Croham Hurst School should be published. With 1999 being the school's Centenary year, the Board of Governors has felt it appropriate that the publication of the school's history should coincide with this important anniversary.

In the book the school's development is placed within the broader context of the main socio-political influences of the 20th century, showing a useful insight into how Croham Hurst has responded to changing ideologies.

Of course, it is the pupils, their welfare and progress, that are the fundamental concern and purpose of a school. Croham Hurst School prides itself on the several thousand pupils who have benefited from the very broad and balanced education that has been provided over the course of this century.

The book effectively describes how Croham Hurst has been so fortunate in having such inspired and dedicated headmistresses and how much has been achieved through their leadership. The general operation of the school is also portrayed, from the very diligent and able teaching staff to the support staff and administrators who also play a vital role in the life of the school. For nearly half a century governors have given willingly their time and expertise for the benefit of the school. To all these people and more, the school is indebted.

Finally, on behalf of the school I would like to thank Mrs. Monica Sharpe for having undertaken this immense task and to express much gratitude to her for her untiring work. I would also like to congratulate her on producing such a comprehensive book for our interest and enjoyment that depicts one hundred years of Croham Hurst School so informatively.

Having been associated with the school in numerous capacities for over half a century, it gives me very great pleasure to recommend this book to you.

Margaret E. Carter-Pegg

MARGARET E. CARTER-PEGG
(née Mant)
Chairman of the Board of Governors.
January 1999

INTRODUCTION

This cannot be the definitive history of the school. Many of the events are too close for a proper historical perspective to be seen and, as a past member of staff, my own view and judgement is inevitably not totally impartial. Most of the original sources were unavailable, the early ones having been disposed of, and the later ones, like govenors' minutes after 1968, being still confidential. The materials that have been available have, however, been tremendously enjoyable. Miss Balcombe, a former history teacher, had written an account of the first sixty years of Croham Hurst which has proved immensely useful. Many people, far too many to list here, have generously given me their time to reminisce about their school days or talk about their work. (One of them, Betty Rogers (Marillier) joined the school in 1908 and was interviewed a few weeks after her 100th birthday.) A band of noble old girls and retired staff have spent years arranging photographs, letters, papers, books and the wonderful Form Books into an orderly Archives Cupboard, in which I have spent many happy hours. Donie Rowlatt and Mollie Christopher have been particularly helpful in checking facts, spelling and style. The Old Crohamians' Association has generously given a donation towards the cost of the book, for which everyone connected with the production of the book is most grateful. Margaret Carter-Pegg has played the most important role of all—initiating, encouraging and completing the whole project. This cannot be the history of the school, but it is a composite picture of the school's first 100 years, and I hope it will bring enjoyment to those connected with the school. Croham Hurst's strengths became more obvious to me the more I learnt about its history. I may be prejudiced, but the pride so many feel in Croham Hurst School came to seem perfectly proper.

MONICA SHARPE

CHAPTER 1

1899-1927

'Footprints in the sands of time'

In 1899 South Croydon stretched no further east than Croham Park Avenue. Beyond that were fields, with Croham Farm at the bottom of what is now Croham Manor Road. Horse buses still ran to the *Swan and Sugar Loaf*. The upper part of Croham Road, and Croham Valley Road and Ballards Way were just tracks. Queen Victoria, on whose empire 'the sun never set', still had two more years to reign. 'Victorian values', which included respect for authority, the inevitability and rightness of class distinctions, and a moral family life were all accepted by most people without question. In this Victorian society most people in the middle and upper classes regarded women primarily as ornaments and home makers whose role was to look good, to run the home, control the servants, and produce children. The skills they needed were domestic skills, and accomplishments like painting, music and manners, which could of course be taught at home. However, as Croydon expanded, mainly with houses for professional people who could use the railway to travel up to London for work, there were girls' schools founded in Croydon, some of them obviously aiming to do more than just teach lady-like pursuits. By 1899 there already existed Croydon High School, founded in 1874, Coloma (1879), Old Palace (1889), Woodford House 'for the daughters of professional men', Aymesby House 'for the daughters of gentlemen only', the Grove House School for Young Ladies, and others.

It was in 1899 that Miss Kathleen Ellis started a little school in Number 59 Croham Road, with five day-girls and two boarders. This was the beginning of Croham Hurst School. It was like a little family, a Victorian family, where authority was not questioned, and where the relationships were expressed in ways that would seem to us today to be perhaps sentimental, even unreal. Even when the school got bigger, Miss Ellis was openly addressed as 'Auntie-Darling' by several older girls who had been her first pupils. Girls remembered her kindness, care and humour. The school grew and expanded into a second house in Croham Park Avenue (number 2 next to the church) and in 1901 Miss Ellis was joined by Miss Theodora Clark. They remained joint headmistresses until 1921, though after Miss Clark's arrival Miss Ellis seems to have slipped into a role more like that of housekeeper and matron than headmistress.

Theodora Clark was by all accounts a remarkable woman, much more academic than Miss Ellis, with positive educational ideas which in some ways ran ahead of the

1 *59 Croham Road, the first school building*

thinking of the time. She came from the Somerset Quaker family of Clarks, best known for Clarks' Shoes—the founder of the firm was her grandfather. She was born in Street, Somerset, in 1863 but her family moved to Croydon in 1864. She went to Croydon High School, and then from 1879 to 1881 she was at the (Quaker) Mount School in York as a pupil-teacher, receiving some education in return for duties. She taught at Sidcot school in 1881-2 and joined the staff of Croydon High School from 1885-90, though she seems to have had no formal qualifications whatsoever on leaving the Mount, not even matriculation. Her next move was to become a governess, some of the time in Egypt. She obviously made a success of this as the daughters of the Potter family whom she had taught joined her at Croham Hurst.

The school flourished under the joint headmistresses and they soon decided to construct a purpose-built school, specially designed to be capable of expansion, but also of being sold as two separate private houses if it fell on hard times. It was built on the present site, then a field full of dandelions further up Croham Road, where the country began—'a healthy situation' as a later advertisement claimed. When it was finished in 1907 Miss Clark and Miss Ellis gave a feast to the workmen, who were waited on and entertained by the girls—an anecdote told with pride, as middle-class girls did not expect to wait on workmen.

Theodora Clark was tall and erect, carefully dressed and serene. Her pupils thought of her as beautiful. It was Miss Clark's personality rather than Miss Ellis's which shaped the school. The two things which seem to have impressed pupils and parents most were her love of beauty and her high Quaker ideals. Appreciation of beauty came across as she taught literature. Girls talked of the way she would 'fire our imaginations and open the doors and windows of our minds'. This was not only in lessons. She would take pupils to London to the theatre. In 1908 they went to see *Twelfth Night* performed by Sir Beerbohm Tree's famous company, not a usual outing for girls at that time. She wrote poetry and plays herself. Each year there was an Exhibition at the school when art and needlework done during the year was on show for visitors. Most years, the play performed then was written by Theodora Clark herself and often directed by her too. In

2 *Miss Clark and Miss Ellis and pupils in the garden of 2 Croham Park Avenue, the second school building*

3 *Theodora Clark*

4 *The new school building of 1907*

1910 one of her plays was put on in the large Public Hall in Croydon in aid of the National Theatre fund. With the emphasis she gave to poetry and drama it is not surprising to find the daughters of the poet Walter de la Mare and the daughter of the Shakespearean scholar Professor Dover Wilson at the school.

To a delight in beauty in literature Miss Clark added an appreciation of art which she longed to share with her pupils. She gave lectures: there was one on Greek Art in 1913. She frequently took parties of girls to visit the London galleries. She would also take parties of older girls abroad, to Florence or Venice or Holland. Few schools then took parties abroad, though it has since become commonplace. Travel was of course not easy in those days. Dorothy Mathews (a Crohamian who had been active in QMAAC in the First World War and became Divisional Secretary for the Red Cross in the Second) had described some of the difficulties of this expedition:

> No sleepers or couchettes, a picnic basket with a spirit kettle accompanied us for journey and picnics. We stayed at a very simple pension with no bathroom, so Miss Clark brought with her a collapsible rubber bath which was nick-named 'the Shell' with apologies to Botticelli's Venus which we had seen in the Uffizi.

5 *The school from the back garden*

The beauty of the buildings, pictures and scenery were Miss Clark's main concern on these journeys, but she was always very concerned about beauty of personal appearance also. In Florence she bought a hat, and asked her pupils what it looked like. They were all complimentary, naturally, as one would be to one's headmistress. When she returned to the pension and saw herself in the mirror, she was quite cross that they had not had the courage to tell her that it did not make her look beautiful. She never wore it again. We see her concern for personal appearance on another occasion, this time the appearance of her pupils, when in 1909 some Croham Hurst pupils went to Paris to sing with the Girls' School Music Union. Miss Clark went with them as chaperone. They visited—of course—art galleries, Versailles, Sainte Chapelle and many other beautiful places. The choir was conducted by Saint-Saens himself as they sang one of his compositions. They describe their preparations for the great event. 'We dressed with much care. Our white bows surpassed themselves. Our crimson roses were patted to perfection and thus pinned on by our fastidious chaperone.' For Theodora Clark, beauty of all kinds was important and her girls must be well dressed.

The other characteristic of hers which made a deep impression on the school was the high moral tone resulting from her Quaker faith. Croham Hurst was not a Quaker school in the sense that the Mount School at York was, belonging to the local branch

6 *Miss Clark (on the left in the front row) with the choir of Crohamians and their French hostesses in Paris in 1909*

of the Society of Friends who appointed the governors. Croham Hurst at this time had no governors. It was the personal property of Miss Clark and Miss Ellis, built with money largely borrowed from friends. But there are many aspects of Croham Hurst in the early days which show Miss Clark's adherence to Quaker principles. The moral seriousness is seen in the articles she wrote for the magazine, always urging deeper thought and better living. There is a book in the archives of the talks she gave on Sunday evenings to the house-girls (boarders). One in 1907 has the headings:

Do not   or Check yourself
Do   or Compel yourself
Be   or We must turn our most vehement attention and our highest
                 thought to those bright things in which self has no part.

Each Friday there was a 'Second Hall', an additional assembly in the last period of the morning. There would be put up on the board at the end of what is now known as the Small Hall a motto or a piece of poetry. Miss Clark would give an improving talk on it, and it would remain there as the motto for the week. These mottoes are collected in a leather bound, gilt-edged book. One well remembered one was 'Politeness is only an air-cushion. There is nothing in it, but it softens the bumps'. The house-girls also had the 'Silence Library'. At 6pm on weekdays a bell would be rung and the House would assemble in the Hall and would read an improving book in silence or just sit in silence for 20 minutes. On Sundays girls who did not attend churches of their own denomination would be taken by Miss Clark to the Friends' Meeting House in Croydon. At school she herself taught the Scripture lessons. So although girls were not pushed into becoming Quakers there was no doubt about the moral stance of the school.

Another feature that Croham Hurst shared with Quaker schools was the lack of competition. Examination success was not emphasised. The annual School Meeting was a Speech Day, not a Prize Day. There were no prizes. What was encouraged was profitable use of leisure. Miss Clark introduced 'occupations'. Everyone was supposed to do something useful and creative with her leisure time. Helen Sandy, pupil, mother, teacher and active Crohamian for 60 years, remembers Miss Clark, who went through each girl's occupation with her, looking at a piece of embroidery she had done and saying, 'It is beautifully worked. Could you now design a piece yourself and then embroider it?' This started Helen on a lifetime of creating beautiful embroideries and teaching others to do so.

Occupations could include almost anything absorbing: one girl bred chickens. Diligence was encouraged: in 1920 Elaine Cortazzi made three complete dresses, two suits

7 *The old Hall*

of pyjamas, two pairs of gloves, purses, pincushions, a trimmed hat, a coat, baby's boots, silver buttons and a silver spoon! But not everything was acceptable. When one pupil made a model of a submarine, Miss Clark's Quaker pacifism got the better of her and she broke it. There were also communal leisure occupations. In 1914 Form IV made a model of the Trans-Siberian Railway in plasticine! In addition to occupations, everyone was expected to read each term the designated 'term book', and each holiday the designated 'holiday book' appropriate to her age. They would be examined on the term book at the end of the term and on the holiday book on the first day of term. The nearest approach to a prize was a book inscribed 'For excellent fruits of leisure' which Miss Clark would give to anyone who achieved six 'excellents' or 12 'very goods' in leisure reading or occupations.

Another feature of the school which owed something to the example of Quaker schools and something to Miss Clark's educational philosophy was the importance of attention to the individual, and the encouragement for each individual to achieve and fulfil her own potential. 'Occupations' encouraged this, as did Miss Clark's personal attention to what everyone was doing. Each term each form had to produce a Form Book, an illustrated and often amusing account of the doings of the term and of the members of the form. Miss Clark went through all the Form Books herself and made comments. Personal attention, of which this is but one example among many, is obviously much easier in a small school, and in 1909 there were still only 74 pupils. Miss Ellis and Miss Clark recognised the value of a small size. They intended to limit it to 90 pupils. 'Why 90?' they were asked. 'Because it is below 100.'

Personal attention and encouragement in non-academic activities are also more important in a boarding school, and some of the characteristics of Croham Hurst School in the early days are due to the fact that until 1961 there were quite a few boarders known as 'house-girls'. They slept in dormitories in the school building. (The present Room 6, in what was known as the East Wing was one dormitory, and there were others on the top floors of the East and West Wings and in the part of the building later turned into Room 8.) House Books were kept, and they talk about the normal events of boarding school life, like buying sweets from the tuck shop, talking late at night, and so on. Every morning before Prayers the house-girls would walk up what was then a stony, brambly lane through fields to Ballards Farm, often wearing galoshes. This was known as 'The Run'. While they were out the House Senior on duty would inspect every dormitory and write down terrible comments like 'This is a fresh and airy dormie, but why does Y keep her letters under her hat?' or 'X has too many hairs in her hair brush', or 'Disorder mark for keeping conkers in Sunday hat'. On Saturday mornings at breakfast each dormitory had to report on the reprimands it had received that week. If a dormitory had been particularly orderly it was awarded a 'Talking Night'.

House Parliament was also held on Saturdays, when seniors and office holders discussed House matters, with a careful agenda and proper procedures and minutes, to train for committee work later in life. Staff and School ate together in the dining room (now the computer room) where there was a High Table for the staff. When Miss Clark arrived for breakfast, the door was shut. One could not be late. The staff would 'dress' for dinner and take coffee in the drawing room (the head's study) afterwards. On Sundays

8 *The drawing room in Miss Clark's day*

the seniors were allowed to invite favoured members of staff to tea—training as hostesses, no doubt. Saturday evenings were the occasion for sing-songs and dramatic performances, organised by 'set' heads. ('Sets' were mixed-age groupings of house-girls.) Pupils speak of how the encouragement for everyone to perform, and the constructive comments Miss Clark gave, increased their self-confidence. On Sunday evenings, before the meeting at which Miss Clark spoke, girls would sing or play instruments or recite poems. Margaret Mabey, at school in the 1920s, describes those evenings: 'Miss Clark, flanked as ever by Miss Lyall and Miss Honey, sat relaxed at the end of our informal circle, with her wool embroidery, and possibly did not know how frightened we were of playing our pieces in her presence.' She describes Miss Clark as 'beautiful too, of course. Who could forget that upright figure, backed by the tall hall windows, snow-white hair lit by sunshine from behind, as she presided majestically … clad in blue draperies with bits of bright embroidery here and there?'

It is a picture of a family, dominated by its head. But the family feeling, cemented by Miss Clark's headship, extended to the whole school, not just the house-girls. As with any group who live and work together, various special words and customs developed. Croham Hurst language included 'scratting' (checking on what was happening in 'rest' or break—it was originally 'bratting' but then this was felt to be insufficiently lady-like), 'anti-prabbling' (picking up other people's rubbish, particularly on the Hurst after a Bank

9 *Miss Clark with a pupil in the old Hall*

Holiday), 'The Pleasaunce' (the open area outside the dining room), 'Olympians' (seniors—juniors were known as babes). 'Rest', the name given to break-times until the 1980s, came from the fact that in the early days all the pupils had to lie flat on their backs in the hall for half an hour. The school was small enough to do things all together. Pupils can remember the whole school walking in a chain following Miss Clark to the top of Croham Hurst and singing there together in a large circle. After a holiday in Norway, Miss Clark introduced 'the Norwegian', a complicated collective song and dance performed by the whole school on the last day of term and at other occasions, often accompanied by Miss Clark on the piano. On Old Crohamians' Days it was sometimes done in the garden, weaving in and out of the pergola. (This was at the top of the bank by the Garden Wing and was destroyed in the Second World War.)

There was a distinctive uniform, the cornflower blue djibbah, rather like the ones worn at Roedean, introduced by Miss Clark when the long dresses which appear in the early photos were recognised as impractical. It perhaps reminded her of the clothes she saw in Egypt, and was very different from the shirt and tie, and tunic or skirt of other schools. Another school peculiarity was the mythical Susannah Phipps, a sort of embodiment of a typical, or perhaps idealised, Crohamian. Miss Clark would talk about meeting Susannah Phipps in the corridor, and learning about something in school life which needed putting right, or something which deserved to be praised. Well-written poems, some written by Miss Clark herself, were said to have been written by Susannah Phipps, and were inscribed in a Book of Honour and read to the school. Gifts given anonymously (some by Miss Clark or by other members of staff) were said to be from Susannah Phipps, and she featured frequently in Miss Clark's daily Assembly talks and Friday talks and Sunday talks and magazine articles.

The loyalty created by this close knit community is illustrated in the School Song written in 1914 by Cecily Mackray, a pupil. It was made particularly poignant by the fact that she was drowned off Singapore in the Second World War.

10 *Miss Clark and Miss Ellis with some pupils in the garden*

11 *A lacrosse team in the 1920s wearing djibbahs*

12 *Cecily Mackray*

A loyal band of members, we
To our dear school united.
To her we have sworn fealty,
To her our troth have plighted.
As firm and strong her buildings stand,
The chestnut standing o'er her,
Around her lies the meadow land,
The wooded Hurst before her.

The healthful winds around her blow.
Afar all ills they carry,
And all who from her walls must go
With lagging footsteps tarry.
Her noble love and helpfulness
Are ties that bind still stronger.
Our hearts we'll leave in CHS
When we are girls no longer.

This song was dropped in the 1970s, not only because the meadow land no longer lay around her, but also because the world had changed since 1914 and schoolgirls now found this sort of extravagant expression of affection embarrassing. This kind of loyalty was however felt by many old girls who came back to school regularly for Old Crohamians' Day, which included lunch, a tennis match, a meeting, supper and dancing, ending with the Norwegian, of course. An Old Girls' Association was formed in 1909, replacing the earlier 'reading circle'. (Habits formed by the term and holiday books died hard.) *The Crohamian*, the magazine, was first published in 1910, consisting largely of articles by old-girls and news of them, as it was really intended to keep former pupils in touch with each other. The first copy had one article on school manners, one on the adoption of the school flower the dandelion, a serious—not to say boring—account of Mendel's Law, a comparison of Norwegian and English girls, an account of the organisation of Sunday Schools, and a list of names and addresses of all former pupils. There was of course a picture of Susannah Phipps on the front, looking ethereal and Pre-Raphaelite, with two small girls beneath her wearing djibbahs and holding hockey sticks. This cover had been designed by Margaret Pilkington, a former pupil who later became the curator of the Whitworth Art Gallery in Manchester.

Loyalty to the school seems to have been felt by staff as well as girls. Miss Clark encouraged a close knit friendship between staff members. In retirement she lived with two former members of staff, Miss Lyall and Miss Honey. Several staff lived in the school building and married teachers were rare. Many teachers stayed for long periods; for instance Miss Lyall for 17 years, Miss Ross for 34, Madame François for 31 and Miss Hazel Inglis for 43 years.

The staff and girls were obviously happy, though today's pupils might find this close community sentimental, cloying and restrictive. Its special character stemmed largely from

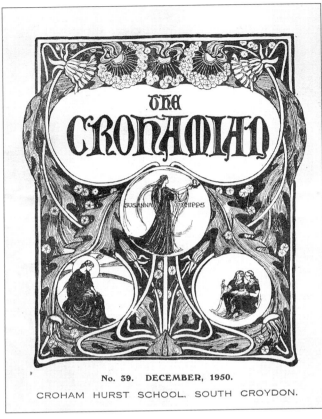

No. 39. DECEMBER, 1950.
CROHAM HURST SCHOOL. SOUTH CROYDON.

13 *The magazine cover designed by Margaret Pilkington*

Miss Clark, her own enthusiasms and her Quaker values. But she was working in a society which had different views on the role of women from our present views. The school was training young ladies in the skills they would need as wives and mothers in middle-class homes. The magazine of 1912 says of Old Crohamians, with evident surprise, 'Many are still needed at home, but a very large proportion have taken up definite work of various kinds'. In the 1913 *Crohamian* Miss Clark writes, 'A girl probably will, but possibly may not marry, particularly in the middle class. Is it worthwhile to prepare for professional work whilst nursing a hope that it will soon be abandoned for home and children?' She answers her own question by saying, 'In voluntary work for the public good there is an increasing demand for trained as against untrained helpers'.

It must have been the thought of training for voluntary work which encouraged many of the activities in school, including public speaking and debating. Girls were expected to be able to address the whole school from a very early age. Debates took place frequently on all sorts of subjects, such as 'A practical turn of mind is a better possession than a sense of humour'. They were not universally successful. In 1923 we read 'This term it was a matter of life and death that the debate should be successful, for Miss Clark determined that no more debates should be held if they were so dull'. They must have brightened up because debates continued. Preparation for the role of voluntary worker was also doubtless one reason for encouraging the Guild of Help. The 1915 *Crohamian* says:

> Acting upon the suggestion of Miss Clark and Miss Ellis that the summer work should take the form of clothes for needy children, some splendid contributions were sent in. Entire outfits have been adapted or made entirely from old garments, all neatly packed in dress boxes. In one box, with two sets of clothes for a boy of nine, were found a hoop and a stick.

Like all girls of the period, Croham Hurst pupils were protected from familiarity with the opposite sex. Barbara Batt, who was at the school in 1925, was once caught

14 *The Domestic School, seen on the left*

talking to a boy over the fence. Her punishment was to chose a sentence from the Bible and write it out 100 times. She chose 'Comfort me with apples, for I am sick of love'.

Of course the role of homemaker was still the primary role. In 1911 a Domestic School was added to Croham Hurst, built on adjacent land on the corner of Melville Avenue. The ground floor had kitchens, a study for the mistress, and a hobby room. The kitchen contained a range, a gas stove, an ironing stove, and clean-scrubbed tables. The adjoining scullery had washing tubs and a wringer. The upper floor contained dormitories, and a classroom for seniors and bedrooms for staff, made necessary by the school's expansion. The Domestic School was not exclusively for existing pupils. In 1912 there were 92 pupils in the main school and 25 additional pupils in the Domestic School, including one married old-girl who had returned to acquire the skills necessary for running a house.

It is not however true that the school was only trying to create a happy family and turn out girls who loved beauty, took morality seriously, and could run their homes well and shine socially. Pupils were prepared for the London Higher Certificate Examination. There seemed in 1912 to be more successes in Drawing Examinations than in Literature or Botany. That year there were five girls in the VIth form. Only two got full certificates. However, in 1913 the school was officially recognised by the Ministry of Education, and the Inspectors' reports were favourable. The advertisement for Croham Hurst in the 1915 copy of the *Croydon Guardian* says nothing about good results in academic examinations, but talks of the aim 'to develop individual powers of mind and character, and train in intelligent habits of work'. It was a very laudable aim, and educationalists of today would approve.

Miss Clark continued to think of new ways to achieve this aim. In 1919, way ahead of the time when such systems became fashionable, she introduced 'Go as you please'. In some subjects, Maths, English and Latin among them, the syllabus was arranged in sections and published at the beginning of term. Pupils then worked at their own pace, passing a test on each section before proceeding to the next. The teacher was there to help, answer questions and give the occasional class or group lesson. There were 'free periods' when pupils worked on any subject they chose, though records had to be kept. This was combined with an 'intensive system': a three-week timetable so that each week would consist of lessons on only one or two subjects. This system was not kept for long, as it did not fit in well with examination requirements, but the fact that it was introduced at all shows that Miss Clark was still, as she neared retirement, thinking of ways to fulfil her educational aims.

The introduction of outside lecturers was another example of innovation, a refusal to remain content with merely doing things in the accustomed ways. In fact, Theodora Clark was not only an innovator, but tried actively to encourage her pupils to develop a 'spirit of adventure', and in her farewell speech told her hearers they should 'embrace change'. Her comment written in an account of the visit to Paris in 1909 shows how she was always trying to develop an all-round education. She writes:

> The equivalent of a year's language lessons has been learnt in a week in the school of experience, which has taught need and desire. 'Experience is a very good school, but the fees are high' says the proverb; and these fees were high, too high for many headmistresses who reluctantly refused for their girls the tempting invitation; it was difficult to adjust timetable, examination work, to arrange for chaperones, to select pupils. Yet for those who risked the experiment, the result was a confirmation of all their hopes. For the best lesson a school can teach is that of the spirit of a community, its privileges, claims and bonds. And this week in Paris meant an extension of the community in many terms of expression.

This extract, in Miss Clark's rather dense prose, well expresses her thinking about education and about the most valuable lessons to give.

15 *The staff in 1926. Left to right, back row: Miss Hutchins, Miss Lapthorne, Miss Cater, Miss Champness, Miss Ross, Miss Honey; middle row: Madame, Miss Thompson, Miss Lyall, Miss Clark, Miss Meadows, Miss Inglis; on ground: Miss Murrle, Miss Berry, Miss Vincent.*

16 *The Belgian boys who came to Croham Hurst as refugees*

Enough people approved of her thinking and ideals to choose Croham Hurst in preference to other schools. The Mayor of York, who was a Quaker, sent his three daughters to Croham Hurst rather than the Mount School, specifically so that they could be taught by Theodora Clark. Mabel Weiss's parents, returning to Manchester to live, kept her as a boarder at Croham Hurst, although there were family links with the Mount—her mother had been the first gym teacher there. The parents of Dorothy and Margaret Pilkington, of the Pilkington tile family, chose Croham Hurst because of Miss Clark, as did Mr. Allan, who was Mayor of Croydon and lived at Coombe Cliff.

Miss Clark's aims and attitudes may have been constant, but society is changing all the time. The First World War changed for ever the secure and privileged existence of the English upper and middle classes, and also society's view of the role of women. This was not immediately obvious in Croham Hurst School, though of course its effect was felt eventually. What was immediately noticeable was the arrival of refugees in the school. *The Crohamian* of 1915 says:

> The presence of three little Belgian boys at C.H.S. has transformed the atmosphere in a most marvellous way. To speak French has become the fashion of the day. One meets quite a junior member of the school escorting a minute Belgian in a sailor suit along the corridor, chatting to him in French as if she had talked that language all her life. Come into Form 1 as an invisible guest. Marcel Guillet, aged nine, is sitting by a fair-haired girl, both intent on a picture book. The pictures are being explained in a charming mixture of French and English … Gaston, the eldest, is in the Lower Third. The wistful expression on his face tells its own story of his recent experience of the terrors of war; but when he is rushing about the garden, brandishing a hockey stick, it is hard to realise that his animated face could ever have looked pathetic. Little Paul is in

the Preparatory ... The manners of the boys are charming. Before leaving school every morning they insist on shaking hands with their Form mistress. Besides our little friends the Guillets we have two Belgian girls, one in the Lower Third and the other in the Preparatory.

As well as receiving refugees, the school also helped in a Croydon Recreation Club that had been started, partly for wounded soldiers. In response to Lady Edridge's appeal for red-flannel bed-jackets for wounded soldiers, Crohamians produced fifty! The girls also dug up the field opposite the school (now the Old Whitgiftians' playing field), and planted potatoes.

It was the old-girls who really experienced more of what the war meant. *The Crohamian* of 1917 reports that 'Phyllis had been married only a few months when her husband was killed. The news of Dorothy's engagement and the death of her fiancé reached most of us at the same time. Essa Hammond has lost two of her brothers.' There are accounts of old-girls driving ambulances near the Front Line, and doing various sorts of voluntary war work. The report also states, 'Many Old Crohamians who have been swept into this work of relief say how very little they realised, before the outbreak of the war, the conditions under which the poor live, and confess their ignorance of methods already existing for the relief of poverty and distress.' Nora Cluff wrote from a Belgian Field Hospital, 'I am driving a small lorry. I fetch stores—bread, milk, potatoes, etc.— parcels and dirty laundry, and am also used as a coffin carter. I fetch the empty coffins, and take them when filled to the village church—a simply hateful job. However, "C'est la guerre!"' Dorothy Morris described in *The Crohamian* work with the First Aid Nursing Yeomanry.

> We had convoys in from the Argonne and Champagne districts. One night 47 came. The little reception hut overflowed. That was a night of work,— preparing soup, washing the new arrivals, temporarily adjusting the dressings of those who were very badly wounded, and generally settling them down to the rest for which they longed ... I should never have got through that night if one of the patients had not insisted on getting up and fetching me hot water.

These were Old Crohamians who had been educated as young ladies! The school however continued much as before, and rather typically celebrated Armistice Day by parading—the whole school—round the garden ringing the school bell.

Events after the war do not show great changes in the school, rather a steady development along the same lines. In 1918 there was an epidemic of Spanish 'flu. It was world-wide and actually killed more people than the war had done. One Croham Hurst girl, Mavis Wightman, died, and the effect of the epidemic was bad enough for the school to divide. Those who had not caught the 'flu worked in rooms hired in Bartlett Street, under the supervision of Miss Ross who had joined the school in 1918. Miss Ellis, who was in charge of the house-girls, the catering staff and the domestic staff and the secretarial work, found the strain of this epidemic too much. She retired in 1921, to run a boarding house in Bournemouth, which she also named Croham Hurst. Miss Clark wrote:

Why does she go? Has she got tired of CHS? No, not that. But you can't have a lynx' eye that sees a temperature on the rise, or an Indian's ear that from the Drawing-room hears a cough in the D.S., without paying a pretty heavy anxiety bill. At Croham Hurst, Bournemouth, the grown-ups will look after themselves.

17 *Miss Ellis*

(The D.S. was the Domestic School, the house on the corner of Melville Avenue connected with the main building by a long narrow corridor lined with boot holes and pegs for coats and hats.)

The school continued to grow in size during these years that Miss Clark was in sole charge. In 1917 there were 115 girls; by 1927 there were 142 on the roll, and this included a few boys in the Preparatory, including John Cunningham, later nicknamed 'Cat's eyes' after his success as a night-fighter pilot in World War II. The bungalow at the top of Pilgrims' Way had been acquired for use as a form room, and two members of staff and two maids slept there. Then in 1923 the Annexe was built in the garden, where the Science Laboratories now are. Various members of staff and girls did the actual building, using professional help only for the roof and the plumbing. Miss Honey, who taught Latin, took lessons from a bricklayer. Miss Clark, who was reputed to have kept a pair of white kid gloves for the purpose, laid the first brick. A few of the original bricks were incorporated into the Science block when it was built in the 1960s. When the Annexe was completed it was used as a form room and studio. The members of the school were very proud of the building they had built for themselves.

18 *The Annexe*

The new Studio encouraged even more interest in Art. In 1915, shortly after leaving the school, Mildred Chamberlain (Hall) gave £100 to be invested 'in the 5%s' to provide an award for art. It is still given annually. Music also became even more important with the arrival in 1915 of Hazel Inglis, for many years leader of the Croydon Symphony Orchestra. She was an excellent violinist who had been prevented by the early onset of rheumatism from becoming a concert soloist. In the school she used her gifts to encourage a love of music, not only by teaching individual pupils, but by solo recitals, concerts with her 'Inglis Quartet', and in talks illustrated by 'gramophone' in Assembly. The 'Grades Competition' was instituted, followed by the Grades Concert, in which the winners in the competition performed before the parents.

The emphasis on games also became more marked in the 1920s, although the school had no playing fields of its own until 1947. Hockey and lacrosse were played on a field lent by Mr. Lloyd who lived in Coombe House. (Part of his estate is now Lloyd Park.) When it seemed that two winter games were too many, a ballot was held, in keeping with the policy to encourage the pupils to take responsibility for decisions. The school opted for lacrosse which has been the main winter game ever since. Miss Clark was perhaps not as forward-looking in physical education as in most other things. To the teams' distress, she insisted that they wore white stockings, not socks, for matches until the end of her time. When the dancing teacher introduced the Charleston, Miss Clark, shocked, forbade it. But it is not surprising that someone who grew up in the Victorian age found not all the changes of the 1920s to her liking.

19 *The tennis team in their white stockings*

The refusal to allow academic competition was maintained to the end. Madge Carver (Lady Colgrain) gave a shield for the winner of the Gymnastic Competition, and Dorothy and Margaret Pilkington gave an award for the best 'occupation', but all that was awarded for academic work was a 'Triangle', 'Five' or 'Star' for the requisite number of 'A's. Miss Clark signed all these personally, in the exercise books. Competition was introduced for the right to wear a blazer, added to the school uniform in 1922. Qualifications for this honour were typically membership of a games team, or success in the Mildred Hall Art award or the Pilkington Leisure award. (Old girls could also have a blazer, with a dandelion embroidered on the pocket.)

Theodora Clark herself decided to retire in December 1927. She bought a field called 'Big England' on Polden Ridge in Somerset, and had a house built right on the escarpment, with amazing views over Sedgemoor. She lived there with Miss Lyall and Miss Honey. Here they entertained Old Crohamians, and entered into village and Somerset life. Miss Clark in particular got very involved with the Quaker Meeting in Street, and in various education committees in Somerset. The house is still standing, though renamed 'Broad Acres'. The garden eventually became filled with predominantly blue flowers—Crohamian blue. It was with typical generosity, firmness and whimsy that Miss Clark encouraged people to picnic in her field, but put up a notice which read:

20 *Big England*

21 *The VIth form in 1928, with Ellinor Hinks in the middle of the back row, Mary Carr on the right of the middle row and Mabel Weiss with the dog in front.*

> People who have pleasant faces
> Do not leave untidy traces
> Of their meals in country places.

The impression Miss Clark had made on former pupils was shown by the magnificence of the gifts she was given by the Old Crohamians on her retirement—a Georgian mahogany wardrobe, a laburnam chest of drawers, beautiful linen, a 'wireless set', and a typewriter. The parents wanted to give a portrait in oils for the school, but she said she would prefer a pencil sketch, with the rest of the money donated to a fund to give help to girls in the school who were in financial difficulties. The portrait, by Francis Dodd, still hangs in the Small Hall. Miss Clark said of it, 'I could wish it were less austere, but if held upside down it takes on a milder glance'.

The special nature of Croham Hurst School, its emphasis on community service, on individual development, on the love of beauty, on the value of friendships was really a reflection of Miss Clark herself. There were girls who went on to achieve positions of responsibility in the academic world, largely in the scientific field, which was odd, since the facilities for science teaching at CHS were so woefully lacking at that time. Among them, one became Head of the department of bio-chemistry at University College London, another for many years Deputy Head of the geological department at Cape Town University, and Vera Higgins (Cockburn) became a world authority on cacti and succulent plants. There was an anaesthetist at Great Ormond Street Hospital for Children and several doctors. Perhaps more typically for Croham Hurst, Margaret Pilkington became Director of the Whitworth Art Gallery in Manchester, Phyllis Potter became Co-Director of the Caldecott Comunity for children from poverty-stricken homes near St Pancras, and Ellinor Hinks became Principal of Nonington Physical Education College. But if the local perception of the school as a place for young ladies to learn social graces

22 *Vera Cockburn*

23 *(left) Margaret Pilkington*

24 *(right) Dorothy Pilkington*

was somewhat mistaken, it was none the less true that the emphasis was on fitting pupils to live fulfilling and integrated lives in society as it then was, and to appreciate the good and the beautiful, rather than on achieving academic success. It was said by the Inspectors, 'No girl leaving this school should find the world a dull place'.

CHAPTER 2

1927-1951

'Time ... runs through the roughest day'

During the 1930s and '40s changes taking place in society impinged much more noticeably than before on Croham Hurst School. It was as well that the next headmistress was one who was 'seen at her best in a crisis'. Berta Humphrey had been chosen by Miss Clark, and spent six months in the school acting as Miss Clark's secretary before she bought the school and took over as its head. She had before this been secretary to the Headmistress of Manchester High School. She did not share Theodora Clark's teaching background but she shared her ideals and her faith, and in many ways the school was unchanged under her, at any rate in aims and intentions. However, the depression of the '30s, the Second World War and evacuation, the changes in examinations and in the administration of the school caused tremendous upheavals.

Eva Morgenstern (Frau Bruck) describes Miss Humphrey as 'a stately, cultivated yet very motherly and warm-hearted woman with dove-grey eyes and dark blond hair, with grey strands brushed back and tied in a bun'. The motherliness is remembered by small house-girls who were sad. Mary Chalmers was crying in bed on her first night as a boarder because she no longer had her teddy. Miss Humphrey heard her and gave her a silky rabbit as a replacement, which remained her favourite toy. The motherliness is also remembered by house-girls who were ill, and were visited by Miss Humphrey, sometimes at four o'clock in the morning, to comfort and attend to them. She did not stand on her dignity as a head, and leave unpleasant tasks to others. In fact, she

25 *Miss Humphrey*

seemed diffident at the beginning, compared to the regal Theodora Clark, but she obviously grew into the job quickly, and was remembered by later pupils as a woman of presence, control and high Christian principles, though Eva Morgenstern also mentions as part of her character 'something of an old maid, a certain prim and proper conventionality which many did not like'. Eva's being at the school at all was evidence of Berta Humphrey's high principles. Eva was Jewish, from Germany and Austria, and a refugee from Nazi tyranny. There were several refugees whom Miss Humphrey admitted, waiving the fees, as she did for some others in difficulties, which meant in effect that she personally paid for them, as the school was her property and her income. So like Miss Clark!

So much else continued as under Miss Clark. The House books continue their reports on boarding life: 'Dirty nails have been noticed too often.' 'Sweet papers must be put into the waste paper basket and not dropped on the floor. Paper hankies are not to be put in the waste paper basket.' Boarding life was obviously still the same! At meal-times girls were still waited on by maids, and members of staff sat at the end of tables and saw that the pupils asked politely for the salt to be passed. Before they could go in to lunch, girls had to have their finger-nails, palms and napkins inspected by the prefects. (This was still being done in the 1950s by the Personal Order Monitress.) When outside speakers came to give lectures, girls were given opportunities to sit at table with the visitor and make polite conversation. Manners were still very important—so much so that Mr. Mackintosh was engaged to come once a month to teach the art of well-mannered behaviour. Eva Morgenstern, who was having to absorb English Christian middle-class customs, found some of this difficult to take. She describes Mr Mackintosh as 'tall and slender, a grey phenomenon with egg-shaped head, covered with grey bristles of hair, wing-shaped narrow brows over a pair of piercing dark bird's eyes and a small pursed mouth so red and heart shaped that we were convinced he used lipstick. He would dance into the room like a ballerina.' Eva was often used as an example of how things should not be done. He would order her to 'leave the room—for ill-mannered conduct' crowing 'OUT!' with outstretched arm and finger in the direction of the door. She objected strongly when he said, 'It is always seemly to leave bits of food on the plate', when she thought of the starving children of Europe. And when he said laughing and crying were both harmful to the looks of growing ladies for these 'displays of emotion' cause ugly wrinkles, Eva could not but remember the many reasons for crying she had seen. 'Smile,' he continued, 'always just gently smile, and just once in a while take the trouble to look at your face in vulgar distortion when you laugh or cry.'

Proper manners were very important to Miss Humphrey, an essential part of the education provided by Croham Hurst School. In a chapter which she wrote for a book about private schools, edited by Trevor Blewitt, she describes both her aims, and her assessment of the special features of the school. Her writing does not have the bite and flow of Theodora Clark's, and one wonders how many people read to the end of the chapter. But her aims are clearly, if boringly, stated. 'Croham Hurst,' she says, 'separates itself from mannerless self-determination.' 'The practice of study, the habit of concentration, of orderly thinking and setting down on paper, intimacy with a good library, are all primarily aids to the development of mind and character.' She talks about 'the endeavour to turn out thoughtful women, makers of homes, serviceable citizens, on their guard against popular hysteria, ... spiritually minded, ready for service, alive to the needs of the oppressed, anxious for the honour of their country.'

The methods used to bring about the moulding of this character were substantially the same as Theodora Clark had used. No over-emphasis on academic study; still no prizes, only 'commended' or 'highly commended' written on reports in red. No real system of punishments; only 'plain speaking by form prefects, staff or the Headmistress', though disorder marks had been used since the 1920s. Afternoons had no academic lessons, only games and exercises, dancing, painting, crafts, pottery, or practical science. Accomplishments were still encouraged, with 'occupations' judged by a committee of staff and representatives of the forms. All instrumentalists were annually tested and carefully graded by a joint committee of music teachers, the grades given corresponding to those awarded by the London Music Board, with additional grades between. There was also an annually awarded Music Cup given in 1923 by Nina Pound and a Poetry Cup given in 1922 by Elsie Straker. Holiday books and term books were continued and were examined, with book prizes given for good work in this examination, somewhat inconsistently since there was no reward for effort in classwork or in academic examinations. Deportment badges, introduced in 1919, were also still awarded, by a meeting of holders, and were suspended if the holders were seen slouching. (These were not discontinued until 1975.) Commendations were read out at the end of term for those who had performed their duties as office-holders well.

Miss Humphrey considered co-operation between girls and staff to be very important. New prefects were elected at joint meetings of staff and prefects, and the staff and prefects interviewed office-holders and made comments on their performance at 'Tribunal', an end of term meeting which came to feel rather like a court of law for those involved. Form Books were also jointly produced by staff and girls. To turn out the 'serviceable citizens' Miss Humphrey was aiming for, debates and discussions were still encouraged, and everyone from the age of 11 upwards had to make short public speeches. There were inter-form competitions in public speaking. 'Visitors generally comment on the atmosphere of freedom and happiness, and absence of self-consciousness ... Girls can be taught to be unselfconscious,' she said. It certainly moulded character, but not all characters wanted to be, or could be, fitted into the mould, and some inevitably found the atmosphere restrictive and claustrophobic. But, for those whom it suited, Croham Hurst was a happy place in this period.

The staff were happy too. Miss Humphrey paid considerable attention to welding the staff together as friends. They still had tea in the drawing room after lunch, and coffee after dinner, always referred to as 'Tray'. She would take them out to the theatre or to Wimbledon. Many staff had stayed on since Miss Clark's time, including Miss Ross, who joined in 1918 and did not retire until 1952, and Hazel Inglis who came in 1915 and retired in 1957.

In 1929 Miss Lyall, Theodora Clark's close friend, Second Mistress and teacher of languages and English, retired, and Miss Ross became Senior Mistress while Winifred Balcombe took over as resident housemistress. Girls were not as frightened of Miss Ross as they had been of the austere Miss Lyall. Miss Ross was a 'character'. Eva Morgenstern writes:

26 *Miss Ann Lyall*

She reminded me in some respects of a sturdy horse as she stampeded about the place. She had reddish wiry hair cut into a fringe that almost covered up her steel-blue eyes. She trotted heavily along the passages, swaying her body, and her voice was almost like that of a man. We respected her, not only because she hissed at us at the slightest sound, and because she challenged us without mercy, but above all because we felt she was just, clever and kind hearted.

She was an excellent form-teacher. Her form, the IVth, in their privileged position in the Bungalow in Pilgrims' Way, always produced the best Form Books. One year they did theirs entirely in cross-stitch. Miss Ross was generous, too, continually giving gifts to the school, including the original hard netball court. She loved games, particularly hockey, as well as her subject, Mathematics. Winifred Balcombe was gentle and kind as a person, though she could be strict and rigid in school. Like Miss Ross, she stayed at CHS for the rest of her teaching life and, like Miss Ross again, she continued to be very involved in the school in her retirement, working in the Library, editing *The Crohamian*, and doing anything she could to help. Her history and geography lessons were remembered for 'laying the foundations of an outlook on life based on tolerance and a sense of fairness, a striving for critical independent thought and judgment, and a sense of human solidarity'. She remembered nearly all her pupils, knew what everyone was doing after they left school, corresponded with many of them, and was visited by some right up to her death at the age of ninety-six.

Numbers in the school continued to grow, though the school was still so small that each pupil had to mark time twice as she went through, spending two years in the same form, the top half of each form moving up to become the lower half of the next form. In 1930 Miss Humphrey bought the Tower House on the opposite corner of Melville Avenue. (It was demolished in 1994 to be replaced with modern flats.) This involved selling the Bungalow, and settling her debts to Miss Clark in order to get the deeds of the main school. The business was conducted,

27 *Miss Ross with her form outside the bungalow*

28 *Miss Winifred Balcombe*

in Miss Clark's words, 'as a civilised divorce'. The anxieties about money for a head who owns her own school are shown by the correspondence about this sale. Miss Clark says, 'I kissed the wall the day I paid off the mortgage'. In the Tower House, Miss Humphrey installed her mother, who got very involved in the life of the school. The house also provided more dormitory space, a craft room, and a library, and a separate area for junior forms, thus beginning the distinction between Juniors and Seniors. The house-girls, with their distinctive blue cloaks and hoods were now regularly seen crossing the road to the main school building.

Miss Humphrey was concerned to react to the greater pressure for examination qualifications. The school continued to enter candidates for the London General School Certificate with matriculation exemption, and the Oxford School Certificate, but now a larger proportion of the girls actually sat these examinations, and there were more successes at Higher School Certificate. There were now separate teachers for Chemistry, Physics and Zoology, though these subjects were not presented at Higher School Certificate level. A letter from Miss Clark says, 'Your exam trends are far better than mine ever were. With a flourish of quite pleasant envy I take my hat off to you.'

Extra-curricula activities continued. Societies included the Safety First and Order Society, the Anti-Prabbling Society, the Natural History Society, the League of Nations Junior Branch and others. In 1928 a school company of Guides was established, for much of its time run by Miss Miller, whom Eva Morgenstern describes as a 'quiet, slight, ethereal creature, with a brown wreath of curls rolled round her head, a high forehead, and large brown dreamy eyes'. It was in Miss Humphrey's time that the annual visit of the VIth form to Stratford was started. The practice of inviting eminent people to lecture at the school continued including, during this era, Professor Dover Wilson on 'Shakespeare's England as seen through Shakespeare's eyes', and the historians A.L. Rowse and Alec Clifton-Taylor, who both later achieved television fame to add to their scholastic eminence.

The 1930s were of course the time of the depression in England

29 *House-girls in their cloaks at break time*

and Croham Hurst could not stand aside from changes in society. The school adopted a little village school at Aberlachan in the Rhondda Valley. The girls used to make clothes for the children of unemployed miners; dresses, nightdresses and shirts were sent and, on one occasion, a large batch of navy knickers, made of a thick material which was very difficult to sew and must have been quite uncomfortable to wear.

1937 was the year of a typhoid epidemic in Croydon, caused by the pollution of the Addington Waterworks, known as Addington Well. One of the workmen making improvements to the system was a carrier of typhoid which he is thought to have caught in the First World War. It mainly affected South Croydon. Nine girls and one member of staff caught the illness. It was a very worrying episode, though fortunately no-one in the school died. Also in 1937, Miss Humphrey had decided to respond to the pressures for more science teaching by starting a building fund to provide a laboratory. A gymnasium was also to be included in the project. Various fund-raising activities took place. The staff played their part by putting on a musical evening, and giving a public performance of *The Critic*. Some of the proceeds however were diverted to contribute towards a hostel set up in Croydon for Jews escaping from Nazi persecution and, before much money had been collected, war became imminent, and the school was into its next crisis.

Miss Humphrey, true to form, had anticipated this, and in 1938 had visited various parts of England, with Miss Ross, to find a suitable place should the school need to be evacuated. Bridge House, in South Petherton, Somerset, was actually leased by her for a year before war broke out. In September 1938, when war seemed imminent, Miss Humphrey decided to take 60 girls, whose parents had specially wanted their children to be taken out of Croydon, down to Bridge House while the rest of the school stayed in Croydon with Miss Ross. In the event, the Munich agreement was signed and war postponed, so they stayed in Somerset for only a fortnight. They found it an exciting fortnight, making up beds on the first night with straw from the stables, which included the inevitable fleas, and eating a supper of corned beef and bread and butter and tea, sitting in a circle on the floor. It was new and different to be ordered into squads of

30 *The Staff performing* The Critic.

washers–up, to go for long walks in the country after lessons, or to be taken by coach to visit the local sights. Miss Clark, at nearby 'Big England', one day sent over some roast joints to help with the difficulties of catering in a kitchen not designed for a school. It was rather like an exciting camp for two weeks, until the threat receded and they returned to Croydon.

By the summer of 1939 it was obvious that war would break out and so Miss Humphrey once again took the school to Bridge House. By now they had acquired proper beds, tables, desks, chairs and books. An 'Aga' cooker had been installed in the kitchen. One father, who was an engineer, even brought down the radiators from the Croydon school and fitted them. The Hall School, Weybridge, which was a similar school with Quaker connections and a care for refugees, whose buildings were requisitioned suddenly, joined Croham Hurst for the first few weeks. In the end Miss Brooks, their head, brought more pupils than were expected, which made things very crowded, and she seems not to have made the careful preparations which characterised Miss Humphrey's ways. The Hall girls' traditions of behaviour were somewhat different from Croham Hurst's, and the arrangement did not work. But after a term Miss Brooks found a house for the Hall in Wincanton. Like many other evacuated schools they did not return to London at the end of the war. The Hall closed in 1983. Miss Humphrey's foresight and organisational skills are shown not only in being so prepared for the outbreak of war, but also in reopening a branch of the school back in Croydon when it became obvious that the war was going to be prolonged, and in re-integrating the two groups at the end of the war. Some other similar schools in the London area failed to weather the changes and pressures of the war and did not continue into the 1950s.

One evacuee describes Bridge House like this:

It was not a particularly beautiful building, made from local Ham stone, but it had a quiet dignity about it, with a long drive flanked on either side with

31 *(above) Bridge House*

32 *(right) Main entrance to what was Bridge House in 1997*

chestnut trees, and windows that looked out onto a spacious lawn surrounded by a ha-ha, and green fields stretching as far as the eye could see, with Pincushion Hill in the distance. I remember feeling slightly overawed when I first went into the Hall and Dining Room at Bridge House because the portraits of the Blakes' ancestors lined the walls. Most of them had rather kindly faces, but a few wore rather stern expressions which seemed to grow sterner as the years wore on.

(Bridge House fell into disrepair after the war and has subsequently been demolished. The site is now occupied by permanent 'mobile homes'. The original entrance has been kept, and the stables, and the large cedar tree, and of course the glorious views are unchanged.)

The evacuation to Bridge House served to reinforce the family atmosphere of Croham Hurst. Even when older girls were billeted in the village of South Petherton, members of staff were with them, their relationships cemented by muddy walks along blacked-out lanes on the way back to bed. One particularly memorable time they met a herd of pigs which had escaped into the lane. Lessons were continued, sometimes in the cellars during air-raids. Science lessons took place in the stables, gym in the garden, using an old cedar tree for apparatus. Children from the village came to join the preparatory classes in the conservatory. Out-of-lessons activities formed the real difference, however. The school acquired 30 Rhode Island Red hens and two cocks, and some ducklings and geese. There were three ponies. Bee-keeping was started, which sometimes involved chasing a swarm in the middle of a lesson. They grew vegetables, chopped wood for fires (wooding service), tried to dig up Roman remains along the line of the Fosse Way which crossed the grounds, started a cycle club, put on a pageant on the lawn about the history of Bridge House, and generally made the best of their country surroundings. Miss Hutchinson, who had taught dancing at the school in Croydon, even travelled down once a week from London to give dancing lessons in Somerset. At the Natural History Club, so inspired were the members by their beautiful surroundings, that as many as 32 papers on Nature Study in Somerset were written and given to the Club!

It was war, with its grim side made obvious as the bombers were heard overhead on their way to bomb Bristol. Older girls helped staff carry the smaller children and their sleeping bags into the cellars when air-raid warnings came. Miss Timewell, the housekeeper, possessor of a large bust and tiny ankles and immense kindness, took a large jar of sweets to hand round on these occasions. Seniors were forbidden to discuss war news in front of the juniors, to protect them. But everyone endured the wartime diet—rabbit and parsnips four times a week at one stage—and everyone was inconvenienced when the Navy commandeered the bus which usually took them to the sea. The organisational problems for Miss Humphrey must have been huge, but she seemed full of ideas of how to manage, how to occupy everyone happily, how to protect them. Most of the girls who went to South Petherton viewed these years in a close-knit community in the country as a particularly happy time.

Even misbehaving was different. There were novel ways of doing it, like shutting Miss Husselbee into a loose-box. Eva Morgenstern describes some of the illegal activities:

> Miss Humphrey had bought some chickens, and hired a gardener to cultivate a vegetable plot, so that we should be self-supporting in meat, eggs and vegetables.

33 *The History Society at Bridge. Eva Morgenstern is on the left*

The territory at the back of the house was overgrown with weeds, thistles and stinging nettles in the grass, with a chicken house in the middle. The hens laid their eggs with a preference into the stinging-nettles. We had made this discovery rummaging in the grass and nettles with a tennis racquet in an attempt to retrieve a tennis ball.

In one moonlit night in summer the idea came to us to search for such eggs and to have a nocturnal meal of eggs in the garden. One girl found an old spirit stove on a rubbish heap waiting to be collected. I pinched a bit of spirit, some margarine for frying and a bit of salt from the kitchen. We waited till the teacher on duty had said goodnight, closed the door and disappeared. Then we took some sheets from the beds, tied them firmly together, and let ourselves glide down into the garden. Outside the crickets and night-birds were chirping, the slender crescent moon hung in the dark universe and a scent of fresh earth was in the air. We crept to the cloakroom to get our gumboots, put them on, and in nightdress or pyjamas, gumboots and gloves we plunged into the stinging nettles. Armed with sticks and a torch, we carefully poked and combed through the grass and nettles, and soon discovered quite a number of eggs. Then we dug out the spirit cooker, and an old frying pan also retrieved from the rubbish heap and concealed under the fallen leaves behind the chicken-house, and the meal was prepared. I have never enjoyed a meal of fried eggs as much as this—though the bread and butter we had salvaged the night before from left-overs to feed the chickens fell rather short of our appetite. Suddenly we heard whispering and soft whistling. Three Free-French soldiers [from a unit stationed in the village not far from Bridge House] stood at the fence. At first we wanted to run away—but then the temptation was too great. The whole affair was quite harmless. They were all quite young and smooth-faced like boys, shy, and spoke very little English. Our French teacher was astonished about the unaccustomed zeal shown by some of us for a time in her lessons. But then the French unit was transferred. The adventure was never revealed and the sudden enthusiasm for learning French died down.

The staff who were with the school in South Petherton also became even more of a close group than they had been before. Miss Rosemary Hamley, then Head of Modern Languages, reminisced about fire-watching duties. No-one wore trousers at the school except for fire-watching duties. Miss Humphrey was held to look very fetching in hers. The watching was done by senior girls and staff in the early evening, but during the night by one of the teaching staff and one of the domestic staff. A camp bed was put in the staff-room for one of the watchers to sleep on for half of the night. Every so often they patrolled round the house and out on to a little flat roof from which could be seen the glow in the sky on the nights that Bath was bombed. Living conditions for the staff were not ideal. Miss Hamley wrote:

> My bedroom had been the butler's. Up a steep flight of stairs leading from the stone flagged kitchen passage, it was so damp that I could not use the hanging cupboard at all, as everything developed a coat of green mould, so I hung my clothes on the outside of the door. For warmth I had a little oil stove with a flat top, on which one could boil a kettle or a saucepan. One of my daytime duties was to clean and refill the tiny oil lamps which lit the passages at night.

The staff, living in these spartan surroundings, and with their pupils day and night, were encouraged to join local societies and play a part in village life. The welcome the school received in the village church of South Petherton and the help given by the Vicar, the Rev. Philip Allan, led Miss Humphrey to join the Anglican Church, in spite of her Quaker background. Miss Inglis of course became an important part of local musical life, Miss Miller ran a guide company, and Miss Humphrey herself became area Commandant of the Girls' Training Corps. But in spite of the local links the school was on the

34 *South Petherton Church*

35 *Miss Ross and Miss Miller with the school bell*

whole a closed society, a close family group.

By 1942 many Londoners had decided that the emergency measures, like evacuation, which had been taken at the beginning of the war, were no longer appropriate, and many parents wanted their daughters with them. Croham Hurst School buildings had been leased to a parent, Mr. Meadowcroft, and he was using it for his office girls in the Sea Insurance Company, as Croydon was deemed safer than central London. But the Tower House was still available and Miss Ross and Miss Crockford (a friend of Miss Ross who had done some of the housekeeping at Bridge House) agreed to reopen it for Croydon pupils. To begin with, there were only 10 girls. Florence Ross would teach Maths and Languages using radio lessons for Science. Then the next week she would travel down to Somerset, to teach Maths there, while Winifred Balcombe would leave Somerset to teach English, History and Geography to the Croydon girls for that week. They travelled on Sundays, and their trains passed each other near Salisbury. One Sunday they agreed to meet, but it was pouring with rain, the station café was closed, and when they tried to take shelter in the Cathedral they found a funeral service was taking place!

As numbers grew in the Tower House, three Old Crohamians, Eileen Wright, Elizabeth Duke Turner and Beatrice Brooks, came to help. They were later joined by Mary Carr and Donie Rowlatt, so the shuttle service was discontinued. However, Miss Humphrey continued to travel up frequently, and after the raids were particularly bad they would lay an extra place for supper in the Tower House because Miss Humphrey almost always arrived, to encourage and support. The Tower House girls were briefly taken down to Somerset, when Croydon was badly affected towards the end of the war, but usually a semblance of normality was maintained. Pupils remember, on arriving in the morning, having to shake hands with Miss Ross, well-built and wearing a tweed suit with pleated-front skirt, and Miss Crockford, distinctly thin, who would both be waiting for them by the garage with Nigger, their black poodle. As always, manners mattered! The preparatory and first form were on the ground floor and the older girls were distributed around the odd and somewhat small rooms upstairs. The garden provided a playground, but there was no Hall which would do duty for Assembly, which was held in form rooms. There was a shortage of materials. New girls issued with shiny red notebooks were envied by those

36 *The Pageant of Britain performed in Bridge House Garden*

having to make do with last year's. Djibbahs were virtually unobtainable and anything blue had to pass for uniform. But the spirit of the school remained unchanged. By the time the war was over there were more than a hundred girls in the Tower House and nearly a hundred in Somerset.

The Somerset girls were given a wonderful last term after war finished. Miss Balcombe wrote:

> We had celebrated V.E. day [8 May 1945] at Bridge House with early morning vigorous ringing of all the school bells, a service of thanksgiving in the village church, a huge bonfire in the evening, fireworks and illluminations in the village and a whole holiday the next day. This started with a staggered breakfast from 8 to 11.30 and ended with a fancy dress ball in the evening.

Miss Humphrey claimed 'educational purpose' to get enough of the rationed petrol to take the school on coach trips to visit places of interest in Somerset. Plays were produced to which the whole village was invited, and at the annual Exhibition (held by the school in Somerset as in Croydon) the pageant of Somerset history which had been prepared in 1940 was repeated. Miss Balcombe again—'The real stars of the scene were Peggy, the surviving pony, the hens, ducks and four stately geese who all carried out the parts assigned to them with perfect dignity and success, coached by small helpers hidden behind the bushes'. The school donated some vestments and a carved wooden stool to the church in the village as a remembrance of their time there. Some girls from the neighbourhood who had attended the school had been so happy there that their parents now sent them to Croydon as boarders, including the daughters of the Vicar of South Petherton. Ann Penny remained in Somerset for a futher year after the rest of the school had returned, teaching the local junior children in the Toc H Room. She not only taught them, but gave them dinner. The local baker would deliver the first course hot, and Miss Penny would herself prepare the vegetables and cook the pudding, which was sometimes 'Mrs. Penny's Best', a sort of bread pudding.

On the school's return to Croydon, Miss Humphrey faced other challenges. Firstly there was the difficulty of getting the school building ready—broken windows mended, drains tested and so on—when there was such a shortage of materials and labour and great difficulties in getting permission to do any building work. Then there was the difficulty of welding the two parts of the school into one. Every person as well as every thing had to be labelled for the first fortnight until people got to know each other and to know their way around. Then, when things seemed to be settling down, Miss Humphrey heard that the boys' preparatory school in 'The Limes', further up Melville Avenue, had decided not to return from their war-time home in Dane Hill, Sussex. Even before the building was on the market she decided to buy it. It had been used by the Army during the war, so needed much repairing. The playing field had been planted with potatoes, and a tree was growing up in the middle of the swimming pool. So the struggle to get scarce building materials, men and licences started again. The Tower House was sold and all its equipment taken in procession up Melville Avenue. The Limes became the junior school. Miss Penny came up from Somerset and moved into the Limes with her mother. Miss Ross and Miss Crockford also lived there, and there were dormitories for senior girls too on the upper floors, as the junior forms occupied only the ground floor. Croham Hurst now at last had a playing field of its own, once the potatoes had been dealt with.

37 *The Limes from the playing-field*

38 *A visit to* MVS Westbank

By 1946 the school had 255 pupils, way beyond Miss Clark's ideal of ninety. Of these 45 were house-girls, many of whom came from Somerset. Miss Balcombe would go down at the end of the holidays to escort them back by train to Croydon. Madame François came back from France with tales of what it had been like to live in occupied territory. The school had lost several good friends during the war, including the Crosfield family, who had died when their house in Castlemaine Avenue was hit by a V2 rocket, and Cecily Mackray who had been drowned off Singapore. (Cecily had written the school song.) But the war soon became a memory, and school life resumed normality. Visits to London for the theatre, concerts and ballets resumed. School societies started again. Performances, speech contests, plays, the Exhibition, all took place as before. Boarding life continued with its special customs, though the expedition to the Sunday service was to the Parish Church, not the Friends Meeting House, and there were additions to the routine, like the nightly escorted walk up Melville Avenue to the dormitories in the Limes. (The Vineyard was a private house still and there was no path through from the main school to the Limes.) In 1948 the school joined the British Ship Adoption Society, and letters were written to the *MVS Westbank*, and visits paid to her when she was in London.

Miss Clark had died during the war, in 1940, and was buried at the Friends Meeting House in Street where her gravestone can still be seen. Ann Lyall, her close friend, decided to give a memorial to her in the school, and in 1948 the stained glass window in the Small Hall was installed. It was designed by Barbara Waller (Batt), an Old Crohamian. It is a figure of St Ursula, an early English princess reputed to have hidden children beneath the folds of her cloak to protect them from a tyrant. It includes as the children figures of Crohamians wearing djibbahs, based on Barbara's daughters and her niece, also

Crohamians, and of course at their feet the school flowers of cornflowers and dandelions. As a further memorial to Miss Clark the Old Crohamians endowed a scholarship for a girl leaving the school to enable her to continue her education at college. The original suggestion was 'to provide a scholarship or bursary enabling a girl or girls in financial need to be educated, or to continue her education at Croham Hurst School or at an alternative school'. But during the war the Old Crohamians' Association was in abeyance, and by 1946, when money was still being collected, and regular Old Crohamian meetings were resumed, it was decided instead to 'award a scholarship to a girl proceeding from Croham Hurst School to university or other place of further education'. It amounted in the early years to £30 for one to three years. The first recipient was Margaret Richter who went to study at Grenoble University.

1949 was the school's Jubilee and also Miss Humphrey's 21st year. It was celebrated with speeches to the whole school on the dining-room lawn from the Head Girl, the Head of House, Miss Ross, and Madame, finishing with the singing of the school song. There was also a special service of thanksgiving in Croydon Parish Church. This became an annual event, the Founders' Day service. In her letter for the school magazine that year Miss Humphrey noted the continuity of tradition in the school. She wrote about:

> consciously living through, with the first Crohamians, the same process of awakening and responding to beauty, developing character and personality, deepening our sense of duty, and experiencing achievement as in those early days. We can still feel the inner happiness that took root long ago, and still flowers among us.

Continuity there certainly was, in tone and aims, in the development of individual

39 *'Save Europe' Garden Party 1948. Note the lush school garden*

personality, in the importance given to manners—'rise to your feet when staff enter the room', 'do not talk or run in the corridor'. But before she retired in 1951 Miss Humphrey instituted a major change: Croham Hurst became a public independent school, with its own council of governors under an educational trust. It was formed into 'Croham Hurst School, Ltd.', a company limited by guarantee and not having share capital. Miss Humphrey handed over the property to the trust, but there was a debenture of £24,000 in her favour, which the governors paid off gradually over the next 30 years. The final payments were made to her estate after she had died. The first Chairman of the Governors

40 *Miss Humphrey in her 21st year with Miss Ross*

was James Patterson, himself a parent of four Crohamians. Other original governors were Archdeacon Tonks, the Vicar of Croydon, Miss Cater, a former teacher at Croham Hurst who had become Principal of Chelsea College of Physical Education, Mildred Chamberlain, an Old Crohamian, Mrs. Conroy Dixon, a former Inspector of Schools, Mr. A. de Jongh, a parent, Mrs. Duncan Harris of the Society of Friends, Sir William Hamilton Fife, the Vice-Chancellor of Aberdeen University and a parent, Mr. Marlar, the Headmaster of Whitgift School, Mr. Marten, husband and father of Old Crohamians and later chairman of the Whitgift Foundation, the Rev. Herbert Stephenson of St Paul's Presbyterian Church, and Miss Humphrey and Miss Ross. No longer was the school under the total control of the headmistress.

Also in 1951, Miss Humphrey became Mrs. Bywater, having married her cousin who was the father of an Old Crohamian. Everyone was pleased for Miss Humphrey as she had lost both her fiancé and her only brother at Gallipoli in 1915. Mr. and the new Mrs. Bywater went to live first in Hampstead and then in Southwold in Suffolk. Like Miss Clark, she kept in touch with the school through the Old Crohamians' Association, and also in her case as a governor until 1968, the year she died. Miss Ross, who had been co-principal for the last year, briefly became headmistress, though in 1952 she also retired. She had been at the school for 34 years as maths mistress and for sometime as Senior Mistress. By the time of her retirement there were 309 girls in the school, but in all essentials it was still as Miss Clark had made it. It was a school where 'fitting' or 'suitable' behaviour was very important and rigorously maintained, but where the development of individual interests and capacities was more important than the attainment of high academic standards, and where the words 'happiness' and 'beauty' were heard more often than 'scholarship' and 'success'.

CHAPTER 3

1951-1970

'Times change and we change with them'

1952 was the year Queen Elizabeth II came to the throne. People talked of a new renaissance, but old films of the time will remind us of how different it was from today's world. Rationing still existed and life was austere for many. Clothes and manners were still formal. Ladies wore hats to all important functions, as pictures in the archives show. Broadcasters spoke as though they had plums in their mouths. There were only about five million cars on the roads (now there are nearer 25 million). By 1970, the first year Miss Seward was headmistress, the world had seen Woodstock, the Beatles and the Rolling Stones, and the development of a different and distinct teenage culture in music, dress and values. There had been a man on the moon and the computer revolution had begun. England had seen a massive immigration of Commonwealth citizens, and a massive outflow of Britons taking package holidays to seek the sun. There was now widespread questioning of authority and of traditional values, as seen in student riots, 'flower power' and the establishment of hippie communes. These are just a few of the enormous changes in thought patterns, values and culture in those two decades. How had Croham Hurst weathered them?

It was, of course, now a differently constituted school, with its board of governors, who took decisions about the running of the school and the spending of money and indeed about the raising of money also. The first governors all had some connection with the school—as parents, former pupils, clergy of local churches, or friends. But they were chosen, as governors continue to be, because they had experience to offer in education or finance or building or some other area of expertise useful to the school. Inevitably their experience made them more aware than some headmistresses would have been of outside pressures and developments. There was certainly no intention to change the underlying nature of the school. The letter which was sent out in 1951 announcing the formation of the governing body emphasises continuity:

> The main considerations are to secure, as far as practicable, continuity and the maintenance of the present policy of the school. We welcome to the Governing Council friends of the school of long standing, who are concerned to preserve the ideals, traditions and independence of Croham Hurst … We know that the School will not only be secure under the care of the Governors, but that it will

be greatly enriched by their wisdom and experience. We are confident that they will share in the friendly association of Parents, Staff and children which has been for so long an outstanding feature of Croham Hurst School.

Miss Humphrey herself had expressed these ideals as 'the emphasis on the building of character'.

The existence of a Board of Governors, or the appointment of new governors, does not in itself mean changes in policy, particularly since new governors have their names put forward by at least two existing governors and the issues they discuss are normally brought before them by the headmistress. One can, however, see the influence of the business background of many governors in the ways that money was raised for the building expansions that were so notable an aspect of the 1950s and '60s at Croham Hurst.

There were some interesting personalities among those first governors. Sir William Hamilton Fyfe had formerly been Headmaster of Christ's Hospital, and Vice-Chancellor

41 *Mildred Hall (Chamberlain)*

of Queen's University, Canada, and of Aberdeen University. He had a daughter who had been at Croham Hurst and who, he claimed, was 'terribly nice'. Miss Cater had been on the staff as a physical education teacher under Miss Clark from 1921 to 1926. She later became Principal of Chelsea College of Physical Education. A later link with this college included Miss Roberts, the school P.E. teacher in the 1940s, who trained there. Miss Cater weathered the difficult years of the college's removal to Eastbourne. Both the college and Croham Hurst were very sad when she died in harness, still a governor, in 1953.

Mildred Hall, also one of these first governors, was one of Miss Clark's pupils, one of the favoured ones who accompanied her on the visit to Florence. She married Frank Chamberlain a few years after leaving school and lived first at Spring Park and then in the substantial and beautiful Glebe House in West Wickham. She maintained a close

42 *Miss Clark being adventurous. Mildred Hall is on her left.*

interest in the school, serving for long periods on the Old Crohamians' Association Committee, and corresponding with Old Crohamians overseas. She herself often judged the entries for the art prize which she had donated shortly after she left school. She is to be seen in an early film in the school's possession wearing a hat and a 'sensible' tweed suit with a skirt just below the knee. She is at Big England with Theodora Clark, who stands upright as ever, but with a skirt down to her ankles. Mildred's unexpected death in 1953 was a blow to both school and Old Crohamians. The mourners at the funeral included the Head Girl and Deputy Head Girl.

After Mildred died, her husband Frank Chamberlain became a governor. He was a solicitor of Lincoln's Inn, and a Freeman of the City of London. He became chairman of the Croydon magistrates, High Sheriff of Kent and in 1952 Deputy Lieutenant of Kent. He had wide interests, in boys' clubs and working men's clubs, in the Young Farmers and Toc H, in dance and fine art. Colonel Chamberlain showed a keen interest in Croham Hurst, becoming Vice-Chairman of the governors and Chairman of the Fund-raising Committee. He continued the Mildred Hall Award after her death, arranged for and donated the Coat of Arms for the School, and in 1958 gave the original capital for the Jubilee Scholarship for a girl from the Limes to enter the senior school. Finally, and most spectacularly, a few years after Mildred's death, he married Stella Wickham, the Headmistress, and lived in the school for part of the time, becoming concerned with day-to-day school affairs. He always wore a cornflower—the school flower—in his lapel as a mark of his commitment.

The first Chairman of the governors, James Patterson, was a chartered accountant by training. He had four daughters, all educated at Croham Hurst, which he had chosen because of the special attention it gave to developing and encouraging each girl's individuality and natural gifts. It was during his time as chairman, from 1951 to 1966, that the biggest expansion of buildings since 1906 took place. This made possible the change in the size of the VIth form, the higher academic standards, and the wider curriculum which were the most noticeable features of this period.

43 *James Patterson*

The buildings of the school were now of course the responsibility of the governors. Plans for expansion went back to the end of Miss Humphrey's time. She had asked for a full inspection from His Majesty's Inspectors, which took place in 1952. Recommendations were made which involved changes to the buildings, and the next headmistress, Stella Wickham, was very keen to implement them. First, however, the land around the Limes was bought. Then in 1953 an appeal for money from parents and friends was launched. The intention was to replace the old narrow corridor running between the main building and the D.S. with new classrooms and a wider corridor. The two classrooms now known as 3 and 4 were built in 1955. While these first changes were in progress, the school received the very generous gift of a library from Mr. and Mrs. Howard Wagstaff, to be built on top of the new classrooms. The inspectors had recommended the expansion of the library, which up to that time had been housed in just a small room in the D.S. (The current upper staff-room occupies the site of the old library and also of two bedroooms for boarding staff—Miss Vernon and Miss Pollard lived there in the 1950s.) The governors had made available funds for new books and shelving, and a small subscription was collected from classes to go towards the fiction books. The gift of a complete new building to form the first floor over the classrooms was beyond the governors' hopes.

Mr. and Mrs. Wagstaff had lost their daughter Elizabeth in a bombing raid in Croydon when their house in Winchelsey Rise was destroyed, while Mr. Wagstaff himself was away serving in the army. The police officer on the scene wrote the following account for the *Croydon Advertiser*:

When I managed to crawl down to the trapped people, I found Mrs. Wagstaff, the occupier of the house, nursing her baby Nicola, another elderly lady, who I understood was the nanny, and a young child buried up to her chest in debris … Mrs. Wagstaff pleaded to be allowed to stay with her young child, but I told her that if she did not get out quickly we would probably all be buried and killed … The concrete roof of the shelter began to slip down. I realised that Elizabeth would not survive, as it was obvious her chest was crushed … She opened her eyes and I said, 'It's all right, love. I will keep the light of my torch on and we shall be all right'. She just smiled and closed her eyes and I knew the end was very near. I had one more go at clearing the debris from her, but it was no good, and by then I knew that she was dead. I built a small wall around her shoulders and face and put my steel helmet over her face to protect it. I then managed to crawl out … The only comfort I could give Mrs. Wagstaff was that her daughter had not died in the dark and alone.

Elizabeth, had she lived, would have gone to Croham Hurst, as did her two sisters, Nicola and Margaret. The dedicatory panel in the library given in memory of her says:

This library is dedicated
in memory of
Elizabeth Mary Wagstaff
and other children whose lives
were lost during the World War
1939–1945
It is given to enrich the lives of those
who would have been their friends, and
to young people of succeeding generations
May God grant us peace
14 November 1956

The dedication was performed by the then Bishop of Durham, Maurice Harland, who had been Bishop of Croydon at the time of Elizabeth's death. In his speech Howard Wagstaff said, 'The greatest reward, and indeed the greatest comfort, we can receive, will be the knowledge that in some measure you may receive from this memorial library something which will always be of use and value to you'. Subsequent generations of

44 *The new Wagstaff Library*

Crohamians have received much of use and value in that room. Until his death in 1994, Howard continued to send a flower arrangement for the library on Elizabeth's birthday, as her sisters still do. The magnificent gift enabled the new building to be two storeys high. Gifts of tables and chairs were made by Old Crohamians, governors and friends, and the expansion of the library contents proceeded so fast that Mr. and Mrs. Wagstaff gave two further bays for books.

    The library provided a good place for lectures. Two were particularly remembered. Colonel Chamberlain arranged for Dame Margot Fonteyn to come and delight the girls

45 *Dame Margot Fonteyn in the new Library*

and staff with her account of life as a prima ballerina. It was also in the library that Lancaster Herald in 1958 presented the scroll commemorating the gift of a Coat of Arms for the school, paid for and arranged by Colonel Chamberlain. The features of the heraldry of this coat of arms refer to various aspects of the school's life. The lion, the emblem of nobility and independence, holds the key of knowledge as he faces outwards towards the world. The blue mantling surrounding the helm is supposed to show that valiant struggles had been fought and won. The cornflower-blue of the mantling was Miss Clark's favourite colour. The lamp of learning is a reminder of the one held aloft by Susannah Phipps on the covers of the early magazines. The tent, or sperver, symbolises protection, and its open flap the friendly welcoming school. The chevron vert is the green hill of Croham Hurst, the sprig of lime, of course, represents the Limes and the grapes represent the Vineyard, the school's two additional buildings. There are dandelions in the design. These had been chosen as the school flower not only because the main building had been on a field of dandelions, but because this flower has deep roots and, in Theodora Clark's words, for it 'the crown is the end, the end which is indeed innumerable beginnings. From the dandelion clock the far-flighting messengers are borne on diverse winds to diverse regions, carrying each the pledge of a purpose and the promise of life.'

    The Vineyard, shown on the coat of arms, had been acquired in 1957 for £4,850. This house, formerly named Woodhurst, owned by the Sandisons whose daughter had attended the school, separated the Limes from the main school. It was nicknamed Naboth's Vineyard in Croham Hurst, as the school had long looked at it with the helpless longing that King Ahab felt for the vineyard neighbouring his land in the story of Elijah. It finally came on the market while the other building plans were proceeding. The governors leapt at its purchase. It made possible the provision of better laboratories for science. The original lab had been the tiny room in the corner of the D.S. which is now part of the working staff-room. Later, Science was taught in the prefabricated wooden building known as the Studio, from its former use as an Art Room, which ran alongside the main corridor linking the school and the D.S. A wooden building was hardly ideal for chemistry experiments. (It was also used for packed lunches brought from home. Each form had to have 'Studio Lunch' one day a week, as the dining room was no longer big

46 *An aerial view of school buildings with the new library showing how the Vineyard divided the site.*

47 *The back of the school showing the Pleasaunce and the Studio*

enough for the whole school. Packed lunch was known as 'Studio' into the '70s, long after the building had disappeared.) With the Vineyard rooms now available, it was eventually possible to offer Science in the VIth form up to advanced and university entrance level. Hitherto the VIth form had normally only been able to do Biology and Physics with Chemistry as O-level subjects and Anatomy as a general subject. Better facilities for Music and Needlework were also provided in the Vineyard and also for Cookery, after a short period in which the present staff room in the Limes was the room for Domestic Science.

In 1958 the governors made plans for extending the dining-room and the Middle House form room by covering the Pleasaunce and including in it a cloakroom. An anonymous gift of £1,000, perhaps from Colonel Chamberlain, covered this. The governors also saw the importance of having the freeholds of 79 and 79a Croham Road (the site of the main school building), and during this year they bought them from Mrs. Glen, the owner of the freehold. They had been held on a lease of £55 per annum up to the year 2002 by Miss Clark and Miss Humphrey. The freehold of the Limes was also bought from the trustees of J.E. Moore. The appeal for funds had raised £15,996 but the classrooms, the Vineyard and all the other expenses had used £13,952, so when in 1959 Benchfield came on the market, an ideal area for expansion, the governors felt unable to buy it. They had already spent more than had yet been received of the money promised for the Building Fund. The need for new buildings was not over, however. In 1961 a temporary gymnasium was erected in the grounds. Before this girls doing vaults in the original hall had to use the 'division room' behind the partition (now room 4) to get a sufficient run, and were liable if slightly out of control to make a thundering descent against the drawing room door (the head's study).

49 *Interior picture of gym*

By 1962 the school could not defer any longer responding to the inspectors' insistence on new cloakrooms. The governors were joined in 1960 by Norman Freeman, an Old Whitgiftian, a wartime fighter pilot, a director of several divisions of I.C.I. and member of various government committees. His daughter was a pupil at Croham Hurst. He was totally committed to the expansion of facilities in the school, particularly where it resulted in the expansion of science teaching. He said, 'We have no future except as a high quality school, and our aim must be to maintain high standards in everything we do.' Of course one did not need to be a businessman to see the necessity. Miss Ayre, the then headmistress, put it like this in the 1964 *Crohamian*:

> To anyone who has had to battle their way up the narrow winding stairs, tried to teach in dark odd-shaped formrooms, and struggled to maintain law and order in dilapidated, over-crowded and leaking classrooms, it was not necessary to explain why the school had to be enlarged and modernised. Ministry of Education Inspectors had gently, but clearly, recommended urgent consideration of these legacies from the past.

The new plan, put forward in 1964 as the 'Susannah Phipps Appeal', was to build in three stages. Stage One required £40,000 for new form rooms in the senior school, cantilevered out over the new corridor, together with cloakrooms, changing facilities, and a covered way. Stage Two, needing £30,000, was for an Assembly Hall large enough to hold the whole school, for new kitchens, and a caretaker's flat. Stage Three, for a further £30,000, aimed at the modernisation of the Vineyard laboratories and an additional form room and some offices. Norman Freeman suggested a new way of raising the money. To quote *The Crohamian* of 1964 again:

It was the firm conviction of the governors that the cost should be borne by several generations. They had therefore obtained with the consent of the Ministry of Education a bank loan spread over eight years, and had evolved an ingenious Loan Note scheme whereby parents could lend the school money at £4:4s:0d per cent, and waive the interest in lieu of fees, which represented a tax free interest on their loan of nearly 7%. As the school is an Educational Charitable Trust we are exempt from income tax, which makes borrowing from outside sources more costly than it would be otherwise. If however we borrow from parents, the transaction benefits the school and benefits the parents by offering a generous tax-free investment.

It required governors of financial sophistication to arrange this. One cannot imagine Miss Humphrey proposing such a scheme, but Mr. Freeman had already suggested something similar for Croham Hurst Golf Club. Stages 1 and 2 of the building scheme were completed together, and by the spring of 1965 the new Hall and kitchens were opened by Dr. Kathleen Ollerenshaw, Chairman of the Association of Governing Bodies of Girls' Schools. The new building had involved the demolition of the Annexe building built by the girls and staff forty years before, and included the covered way joining the main school to the new buildings.

With his interests in I.C.I., Mr. Freeman was particularly committed to the expansion of science education. In 1966 he became Chairman of the governors on Mr. Patterson's retirement. He was very enthusiastic to alter Stage 3 and revive the earlier plan to build a block of science laboratories between the Assembly Hall and the Vineyard, plans which had been dropped when the Vineyard was purchased. Obviously, purpose-built labs planned for separate subjects, with appropriate preparation rooms, would be much better than the converted rooms of the Vineyard. The success of the appeal made this possible and the new labs were opened in 1968 by Sir Ronald Holroyd, formerly vice chairman of I.C.I. 1968 also saw the improvement of the VIth-form rooms and the establishment of a separate VIth-form library, equipped with money given by former pupils and friends of the school in

50 *Aerial picture showing the new hall and covered way and gym.*

51 *The new Assembly Hall with Miss Ayre on the platform*

52 *Aerial photograph showing the new labs*

53 *Sir Ronald Holdroyd at the opening of the new labs. Norman Freeman is sitting on his right and Miss Ayre on his left.*

memory of Mrs. Bywater (Miss Humphrey), who had died in this year. The school buildings were now much more modern, and, since the former dormitories were now available as teaching space, considerable expansion of numbers was possible. Boarding had ceased in 1961.

The work of the governors, of course, was not confined to raising money for new buildings, but their influence on educational policy or the day-to-day running of the school is less easy to trace than their influence on financial decisions. The Finance sub-committee and the Appeal sub-committee had been set up soon after the Governing Body itself, but the Education sub-committee was not set up until 1963. It was intended to be available for advice to the head, and to give a ruling where necessary on matters like selection, entry, the curriculum, discipline, teaching-staff and the provision of books. Where matters of educational policy were discussed by the governors in these early years it seems to have been largely in response to the headmistress's suggestions or the inspectors' reports. It was the inspectors' suggestions in 1951 which led the governors to agree to Miss Wickham's request for 35 or so extra lessons to be timetabled each week. This involved taking in a new parallel form at the Lower IIIrd in the Limes to cover the cost of the extra staff needed.

The greatest change of all in these years, the decision to end boarding, was also taken partly in response to the Inspectors' Report, this time in 1960. This had pointed out the inadequate accommodation for boarding, particularly in the cloakroom provision and in the lack of adequate leisure areas. (Not that the boarders themselves noticed that they had

54 *The interior of the new labs*

any leisure. Saturdays went from shoe-cleaning to prep., pocket money, matches, walk, letter-writing, and 'occupations' in the Hall while listening to classical music.) The headmistress, by now Miss Ayre, asked the governors their opinion on whether, in view of 'the present overcrowding and the demand for day girls' places, it was advisable to continue to take boarders'. She also suggested taking two streams right through the school, though she wanted their

I *The window in the small hall in memory of Miss Clark*

II *The Coat of Arms*

III *Miss Clark and the Venus de Milo in the Louvre*

IV *The collapsible bath in Florence*

After a long, grim, battle the big trunk is at last closed. We prepare to leave sighs of relief. WHEN — the collapsible bath appears on the scene !!!

VOLENDAM

WE HASTEN PAST THE DUCKFARMS WITH THE GREATEST POSSIBLE SPEED!

V *Going past the duck farms in Holland*

VI *'To the Baths' from a 1930 Form Book*

VII *'In the hall' from a 1930 Form Book*

VIII *A-level Textile work, 1997*

opinion on whether it should be the school's policy to have one large form in each age group or two smaller ones. The governors agreed, not without some unhappiness, that the school should cease to take boarders, and that it should take a double stream if there was sufficient demand.

The last of the boarders who had come from Somerset with the school on its return to Croydon had now left, which made the decision to end boarding easier. The decision was also influenced by the fact that the boarding side was running at a loss. Boarding for girls was anyway less popular in the freer climate of the time. The sort of rules deemed necessary to protect girls seemed very irksome. Some remember with distress the rule that boarders must always wear school uniform, even when going on expeditions with their family members. Others remember with amusement how the mistress in charge of a crocodile of boarders would stop the traffic to get the girls across the road, if a file of Whitgift boys was seen approaching, to avoid any possibility of a meeting. These precautions and others like them, which would have seemed normal to girls in the '30s, seemed outrageous in the '60s.

The governors also decided that the school should continue to take girls under seven, and boys too, as in the early days, should there be any demand. The governors decided to award a Governors' Scholarship to a girl going into the VIth form who would not otherwise be able to stay on, and to give a bursary, or in some years more than one, to a girl joining the school from the Limes. They even pronounced on whether hats should continue to be worn. All these matters would have been decided by Miss Clark or Miss Humphrey alone. The governors were prompted by the much more detailed inspections of these years, and were obviously prompted also by the heads' initiatives in some of these issues (not it would appear, the hats), but the decisions were theirs.

What else, apart from the decision making, changed in the school in these years? The ethos of a school depends on more than its facilities, and a large-scale change in staff can alter the whole tone of a school. In the 1950s several long-standing teachers who had contributed a great deal to the school in its social life and attitude, as well as in the classroom, retired. Miss Balcombe, who in addition to teaching History and Geography, had been a selfless mistress in charge of the House, and had played a large part in the drama productions, went in 1950 after 23 years at the school. Miss Ross had dominated the Maths teaching for a long time. She retired in 1952 after a year as head. Miss Miller, head of English and, in her last years, Second Mistress as well, went in 1954. Hazel Inglis had a passion for gardening and bee-keeping. The school always enjoyed her accounts of her early days as a suffragette. She would describe how, armed with a hammer, she broke a shop window in Piccadilly and was taken to Holloway prison where she met Dame Ethel Smythe. When she retired from running the music department in 1957 it was indeed the end of an era. She said, 'During my 43 years at the school, I had the privilege of helping to educate three cousins, one nephew, five nieces and one great-niece.'

These veterans were replaced by others whose contribution to the school was different. Mary Carr (now Mrs. le Fleming) had been at the school as a pupil in Miss Clark's day and subsequently as a piano teacher. She now took over the music department and built up a highly skilled madrigal choir which frequently won competitions, especially

55 *Mary Carr in 1950*

at the Purley and Coulsdon Music Festivals. Miss Rowlatt, with her insistence on high standards and her care for individual development, took over the English department. She had a suitable Shakespearean quotation for every event! Pauline Cockrill, who later became an author, said of her, 'She was my hero and inspiration', sentiments echoed by another author, Jane Waller, and many other past pupils whom she taught to appreciate literature. Miss Porten not only took over the maths department but became Second Mistress, a job which became much bigger as the school grew. Mrs. Williamson came as the head of the rapidly expanding science department. She was particularly keen to develop links between subjects, and make sure that science teaching was promoting not just skills but an all round education. Mrs. Mellor took over the modern languages department after Miss Hamley's retirement, again emphasising not just the language but European culture. Mrs. Plumstead became queen of the newly expanded Domestic Science kitchens, was in charge of careers advice, and she remained, getting involved in the gardens and many other things, until 1979. Mrs. Lucas, Miss Balcombe's replacement, not only expanded the History department (it came to include both Sociology and Politics), but also as VIth-form tutor played a leading part in the establishment of the Contemporary Studies course.

This course was done by everyone in the VIth form, regardless of their A-level subjects. (A-levels had replaced the Higher School Certificate in 1950.) It was planned to provide an understanding of the 20th century in Literature, Science, Philosophy,

56 *Miss Porten singing 'Auld lang syne' at OC Day. She is seventh from the right wearing a cornflower.*

57 *Mrs. Mellor, Mrs. Plumstead and Miss Rowlatt with Betty Moore, the head's secretary in an apron at a 'sale'*

Sociology, Religion, Music and Art, and the links between them. The educational world was at this time becoming alarmed at the dangers of specialisation. Some people, responding to what Harold Wilson called 'the white heat of the technological revolution', seemed to become concerned simply for their own specialities and knew little of what was going on in other fields. The Contemporary Studies course was to guard against this at Croham Hurst. It was not for examination, but for education. In 1960 there was also a separate course for girls in the VIth form who intended to stay for one year only. It included a one-year O-level course in Human Biology, a study of Sociology, and many outside visits. This is the account in the 1964 *Crohamian*:

Tuesday afternoons of the past school year have found the Lower VIth General travelling to many different parts of London and Surrey. One of the most beneficial aspects of the visits has been the wider knowledge gained on the kinds of jobs which many people do; for example we have seen people working on the factory floor at Ford's of Dagenham; at Lyons, Cadby Hall, we witnessed women rolling out 40 miles of Swiss roll; at the Moon Press, Reigate we saw the unique system of printing books for the blind. We have asked firemen, sewage workers and telephone operators about their work. Of special interest to those thinking of nursing or social work were expeditions to Queen Victoria Hospital, East Grinstead, where we learnt many

58 *Mrs. Kathleen Lucas*

interesting things about plastic surgery and its growth during the war period,
and to Warlingham Park Mental Hospital, where our eyes were opened to the
advantages of an open and progressive hospital. An interesting exchange experiment was made between our VIth form and that of Kidbrooke Park
Comprehensive School for Girls. Both sides discovered the advantages and
disadvantages of a very large and a small individual school. At Carew Manor
School, we talked to and learnt much of the work being done for educationally
subnormal children and we found much more similarity with ordinary schools
than we had expected. Other visits included exhibitions in London, the Stock
Exchange, the National Dairy Centre and the Whitgift Almshouses and Old
Palace, Croydon.

All of these were of course in addition to the visits open to the whole VIth form which
included the traditional weekend in Stratford-on-Avon, a trip to Holland, a party to Paris,
a geography trip to Wales and cookery expeditions. All of this depended on an enthusiastic staff with initiative and the capacity to cross the boundaries of their own subjects.
This of course was not new in Croham Hurst.

One new change in the staff in this period is the appointment of more married staff.
This was due to changes in society around and also to the general shortage of teachers
at this time which led to the Government positively encouraging teachers to go back to
work after leaving to have their families. Married staff, however, are less likely to want
to do weekend duties in a boarding school, so this change in society also played a part
in the decision to give up boarders at Croham Hurst. It was also true that fewer parents
wanted their daughters to leave home, again because of a general shift in public opinion.

However important outside pressures, changes in organisation, new buildings, new
staff, and a general change in values and expectations are in shaping a school, there is no
escaping the fact that the greatest single influence on a school is the head. It is the head
who appoints the staff, presents issues to the governors, implements the decisions of the
governors, deals with matters of discipline, balances the curriculum, manages the staff, and
is the visible face of the school in assemblies and all public occasions. During this period
of rapid change there were two headmistresses of Croham Hurst with very different
personalities, each making their distinctive contribution to the school.

The first of them, Stella Wickham, was head from 1952 to 1959. She had come to
the school through a personal contact with Miss Clark in Somerset some years before.
Her vision of the school was, she said, 'of a house in a pleasant garden. A place where girls
acquired a generous progressive outlook on life, where they accepted quite naturally the
ideal of service to the community and where their individuality was cherished tenderly.'
In addition to this rather idyllic vision, however, she obviously also had a vision of how
it could become a more academic place. In 1952 there were only three passes at A-level
in the whole school. Miss Wickham had taught at Abbots Bromley and Cheltenham
Ladies College, and was herself an Oxford history graduate and hockey blue. When she
came to Croham Hurst, it was, for the first two years, as a history teacher, and pupils
remember her lessons with enthusiasm. She had a great interest in architecture as well as
political history, and was made a fellow of the Royal Society of Arts. Although she wore

good quality clothes, her red hair was often all over the place in typical 'blue stocking' fashion, and she would enter a door sideways preceded by a handful of tiny pieces of paper, which would often flutter to the ground at a crucial moment. When she had absorbed the distinctive ways and customs of the school under Miss Humphrey and Miss Ross she then took over as head.

Her seven years saw some radical changes. She it was who suggested to the governors taking in an extra form at the level of the Limes Lower IIIrd, and she was very enthusiastic about the building programme, realising that an increase in numbers was necessary if the VIth

59 *Miss Wickham and Miss Penny dancing 'the Norwegian' at OC day. Miss Wickham is in the spotted dress.*

form was to have a more academic complexion. In 1953 the production of the Form Books, which had provided such an interesting record of termly activities and the characters of pupils, was discontinued. This same year Miss Wickham tried the experiment of an Open Day, instead of the Exhibition with its emphasis on art, music, drama and 'occupations'. Actually this experiment had to be abandoned as the cramped conditions and rebuilding operations made it impossible to accommodate extra people in lessons. 'Lists', the reading of commendations and music and art awards, which was held at the end of term (since 1947 separately for the Limes) was in 1953 held in the evening in St Peter's Hall in Ledbury Road, so that fathers could attend. 'We miss the delightful informality of the garden', said Miss Wickham's letter in *The Crohamian*. This change was, however, moving closer to the sort of Prize Giving which was normal in other schools. In 1955 Miss Wickham went all the way and introduced school awards for academic work and a formal Speech Day and prize giving. At the first of these the speaker was Robert Birley, the Headmaster of Eton.

Stella Wickham was not a Quaker, and had no inhibitions about introducing competitive awards for academic work if this raised academic standards. Under earlier heads the only awards had been for music, or poetry, or sport. The A-racquet awards were given by the Old Crohamians, and the B- and C-racquet awards by various people; Mrs. Smith, Miss Champness, Colonel Chamberlain and in most years Susannah Phipps. (This award was originally an actual racquet. The prize remained at two guineas long after this had become insufficient to buy a racquet.) As late as 1950, when Miss Ellis, still alive though confined to her cottage in a Suffolk village, wanted to mark the Jubilee, she gave a cup for 'occupations' to replace the earlier Pilkington award. Now, when there was an opportunity for a new award—in memory of Ann Lyall, a friend of Miss Clark's who had taught

English, French and German at the school—it was given for distinction in English; that is, for an academic subject.

Croham Hurst became more like the other schools in which Miss Wickham had taught with the introduction of the House system in 1953, giving opportunities for competition in Drama and Sport. Miss Wickham was an indefatigable attender at matches, getting very excited when the school's honour was at stake. She also introduced a new and less idiosyncratic winter uniform. The Carol Service was at this point held in a church, St Paul's Presbyterian Church, as it still is. Boarders used now to attend St Peter's Church on Sunday instead of making the long trek to Croydon Parish Church. Miss Wickham herself would arrive at church on her bicycle with her pug dog sitting in the basket in front. She later acquired a car which she drove so erratically that some on the road felt the old method of transport was better. The only occasion held in the Parish Church was now Founders' Day. Molly Vernon remembered 'the whole school used to walk down to the Parish Church on Founders' Day and on the way the crocodile passed a small shop with a chewing-gum machine outside. The obtaining of this substance became a fine art—one girl put in the money and the next took out the gum, all the way down the column.'

The increase in numbers and the increasing opportunities for women prompted Miss Wickham to arrange a careers room and a member of staff with responsibility for careers advice. Miss Porten was the first. There had been overseas exchanges before, the first one being a joint one with Croydon High School to Sweden in 1949. Now there were German exchanges, French exchanges and Geography field trips. 1958 saw the first full-scale Shakespearean production. All these changes were part of Miss Wickham's efforts to bring the school more in line with other academic schools.

Another change made partly under Miss Wickham's influence was in the criteria for the Theodora Clark Scholarship. As County Awards were now available for further education, Miss Wickham felt it would be more sensible to give the Theodora Clark Scholarship to girls still at the school whose parents were having difficulty with paying the fees, particularly since the school made a contribution to the fund. Miss Wickham's suggestion was not accepted by the committee, but they did decide to manage without the school's contribution and to use the fund from 1958 onwards to allow a girl leaving school to travel abroad when leaving or at any time while at college; 'to plan and embark on various projects which they might not otherwise have undertaken, in the enterprising spirit which Miss Clark herself fostered so wholeheartedly.' Over the years it has been used for things as various as an expedition with the British Schools' Exploration Society to the Yukon, organ lessons, a visit to a school in Kenya, and a parachute jump for charity. An appendix to this book is the account written by Sarah Burns of the use she made of this grant to visit India in 1990. All the emphases in this account, on beauty, on adventure, on entering into new experiences and understanding different people would have pleased Miss Clark enormously.

Some traditions were still kept. Miss Wickham valued tradition in spite of her desire to change so much. There was still Second Hall on a Friday and still the weekly motto on the wall blackboard under the round window in the Small Hall, though it was less noticeably Quaker in tone. 'Manners maketh man' was a favourite with Miss Wickham, as it had been with earlier heads. 'Triangles' and 'Fives' still existed. Susannah Phipps was frequently invoked. Indeed, a Susannah Phipps doll made by Miss Miller lived on the chest in the drawing room. The school still had the house-girls (boarders), seniors sleeping in the attic rooms in the Limes and juniors in the main school building. Together with other staff, Miss Wickham lived in the school. In fact she followed tradition in bringing her mother to live in the school until her death in 1953. Both Miss

60 *Ann and Kay Penny with their mother in the Limes garden. The bungalow is in the background.*

Humphrey and Miss Ann Penny, head of the Limes, had had their elderly mothers living in the school with them. Miss Penny shared a bedroom with her mother, and their sitting-room was where the Limes staff took their coffee break. (The Head of the Limes now uses it as her office.) In addition to the pug dog, Miss Wickham also kept a budgerigar in her room, which she claimed to have taught to say 'Croham Hurst School'. One could arrive at the door to be confronted with a notice which said 'Beware! Cage open'. So there was still a family feel to the school, though Miss Wickham had given academic achievement a much higher profile.

Miss Wickham's last year at the school was an unusual one. Her unexpected marriage to Colonel Chamberlain, vice-chairman of the governors, presented her in some respects with divided loyalties. They got married one weekend, keeping it a secret from the school. She was back, taking Assembly, by the Tuesday, having had one day's honeymoon. Of course, Colonel Chamberlain was very interested in the school, and his generous gifts to the school continued—a House Pets Cup, a celestial globe, a House Cup for work and conduct, the Jubilee Scholarship, invitations for the house-girls to tea at Glebe House. But the new Mrs. Chamberlain was head of a boarding school, responsible for the pupils by night and by day. Now she had a husband to be responsible to, and this was in the '50s, when married women carrying responsibility outside the home was not the norm it has since become. Colonel Chamberlain's first wife, Mildred Hall, had been a full-time wife. It became increasingly difficult for Stella Chamberlain to balance her responsibilities to the school with her duties as a wife. Never a calm and impassive person, she seemed now to find it more difficult to make the necessary independent decisions without her husband, or to exercise the dignified, unflappable poise necessary for a head who is the last resort in matters of discipline and administration. Rather suddenly it seems, in 1959, the year of the School's Diamond Jubilee, she decided to retire. She remained in the district, living at Glebe House for some years, but after Colonel Chamberlain's death in 1970 she moved to Somerset where she died in 1983. She seems not to have tried to maintain the close links with the school that Miss Ellis, Miss Clark and Mrs. Bywater had done, but of course it was never 'her' school in the sense that it was theirs.

61 *The Diamond Jubilee. Mrs. Williamson, Margaret Woodgate of the OCA, Mrs. Bywater and Mrs. Chamberlain are at the table. Colonel Chamberlain is behind his wife, and Sir William Hamilton-Fyfe is on her left.*

The next headmistress, Molly Ayre, had been a head before, at Jersey Girls High School and at Derby School for Girls. She had just spent a couple of years in New Zealand looking after the children of her sister, who was seriously ill. This was typical of her unselfishness. Everyone who knew her spoke of her kindness. Members of staff who were ill would sometimes find half a dozen eggs on their doorstep. Girls working on cataloguing the Library would find that a large bowl of strawberries had suddenly appeared for them. Once when an appeal was made for used clothing for refugees, Miss Ayre, discovering she had several coats in her wardrobe, gave away the newest and best, keeping only the oldest one for herself. Miss Ayre did not have the opportunity to get used to Croham Hurst ways as Miss Humphrey and Mrs. Chamberlain had done, since Mrs. Chamberlain's retirement had been so sudden and unexpected. In fact Miss Ayre remembers being 'given a dictionary by the IVth form telling me why we eat in the Studio, paint in the Annexe, find the VIth form and staff-room in the Domestic Science house, and cook in the Vineyard'. These cannot have been the only features of Croham Hurst she had to learn quickly. Miss Ayre does not seem to have come with preconceived ideas of how she wanted to change the school. She seems, however, to have had an instinctive knowledge and understanding of people and seemed to know all about events before anyone told her. When interviewed at her home in Oxford two years before she died in 1997, Miss Ayre said that, as far as she remembered, her aims were simply to do what seemed to be the right thing and to get people to work together.

Her time as head saw many changes, again, though she seemed to arrive at them by responding to the situation rather than by looking for change. The end of boarding, precipitated by the inspectors' report, and the governors' appreciation that the financial situation made it impossible to provide the sort of accommodation now considered necessary for boarders, was carried through by her. Miss Wickham had been an enthusiastic and energetic fund raiser for new buildings. It fell to Miss Ayre to cope with the major disruptions caused by the biggest rebuilding—the Assembly Hall and labs. She describes the difficulties somewhat wryly in *The Crohamian* of 1964:

62 *Miss Ayre*

Things began to happen in the Christmas holidays when our temporary cloakrooms were pulled down in readiness for our new cloakrooms and formrooms. After the Easter holidays we took possession, through the Music room as our main entrance, of one new cloakroom and one new formroom, while our main corridor was cut in half, sealing off the builders and our back premises from sight if not from sound. Forty-five Upper IVths shared a form room for two terms, and, despite their large and healthy physique, organised themselves with the help of the P.E. staff, who happened to be their form-mistresses, with the greatest of competence … During the Spring term we kept our clothes in various corners. After Easter, our new cloakroom with 150 pegs and lockers seemed quite wonderful. The Summer holidays saw the transformation of our cookery kitchen into a VIth-form science laboratory, albeit as yet equipped in Roland Emmett fashion, whilst the Limes kitchen became a larger and lighter cookery room … This term too we are holding Prayers much as Miss Clark must have done in the original small hall. Only four forms can get in at a time so we take it in turns.

A later magazine reports further changes:

In the Senior School the staff rest-room has been relegated to the attics. Their cloakroom disappeared into the building site, and has re-emerged over the main entrance. Their possessions have undergone burial under dust, and at times we feared the same fate might befall them, especially when a new telephone system wrought havoc with our communications. The Limes have shared our 'remue-menage', taking their attic to make available a room for Mabel [Mabel Waite, the much loved matron] whose bedroom and sickroom gaped wall-less and floor-less under the Middle House roof which later appeared to hang for a time from the sky. The Art room once again has had to divide its time between the attic and the Annexe.

The mention in these extracts of the attics reminds us that these had formerly been dormitories, and all the dormitory accommodation had to be altered. Miss Ayre, Miss Penny, Miss Meadows (head of the Limes after Miss Penny) and Mabel continued to live in the school for a while after the last boarding pupils had gone. They were therefore on site for another great excitement, the fire of 1962. Here is Miss Ayre's account:

FIRE FIRE!

I wonder how many people heard on the South East Regional News of Monday, 6th February, the announcement that Croham Hurst School had been on fire, and that the Headmistress and Caretaker had escaped unhurt? (Mabel, presumably, was burnt?) But, of course, the school knew long before that, when Monday morning's entry to the Middle House was barred and an all pervading smell of burned wood and paint greeted everybody at the door. Looking up, they would have noticed the hole in the roof and felt the icy blast that blew through it down the stairs.

That was an exciting night for the H.M., Caretakers and Mabel. In the middle of our beauty sleep, at one o'clock, there was a violent banging on the door and when I opened it, wondering whether somebody had broken in, or whether war had broken out again and a landmine had buried itself at our gate, Mr Wright and a policeman woke me up with a jerk. 'The Art Room is on fire, and the Fire Brigade is on its way!'—and sure enough I could hear that frightening roaring crackle that a big fire makes, coming from upstairs.

In thirty seconds I was clothed, warmly if not elegantly, and in two minutes the Fire Brigade had arrived, dashing upstairs with a great clatter of boots and apparatus. Hoses were turned on from the two great shining fire engines outside, and Mabel and I descended to the Kitchen to make a cup of tea.

I think Mabel made cups of tea for the next two hours, as the firemen had quite a tough job tackling the fire. The flames, fanned by the tremendous gale, licked their way along our intricate roofing and proved very recalcitrant … Then—miraculously—the WIND DROPPED—quite suddenly … I was watching from the road and almost at once the flames turned to smoke and then that too disappeared.

We spent the next few hours, almost until breakfast time, clearing up the mess, although the firemen were simply wonderful, some of them mopping up the water in the hall as it fell through the ceiling. But, oh, the Art Room, our beautiful new Art Room, with all the loving care Miss Winn had just spent on it!

A fire is no respecter of persons. Miss Winn lost a number of precious things of her own, some of which were the fruits of a number of years' experience. Although our Insurance company paid up … it could not replace such intimate loss, nor avoid the many art lessons in the cramped cold Limes Annexe or Pavilion. And what a mess to clear up. Upper IV.J who moved their form room to the Hall were splendid. I believe they found the interruptions helpful to the learning of rather boring French and Latin verbs. All except five of our old and battered desks were unscathed. Next time I am going to start the fire myself—in our cloakroooms when most of the older desks have been stored there for mending, one day in the summer holidays. But, of course, I shall arrange for the Fire Brigade to come up before anything else is touched.

Responding to crises with good humour was one of Miss Ayre's strengths, and of course she was helped by the efficient organisation of Nora Porten. Her other great strength seems to have been to give such encouragement to those under her that they felt free to suggest changes, and implement them. This was the time when new experiments in teaching, the wide use of visual aids and equipment, the development of inter-disciplinary studies, the increase in Field Courses and visits took place. Members of staff look back to the daily after-lunch coffee and tea-time sessions in the drawing room as times when cross-fertilisation of ideas happened, not simply times when matters of discipline and administration filled their minds.

Miss Ayre was also receptive to new ideas from the girls. It was while she was head that the School Council was formed in 1965, to discuss ideas put forward by the pupils. The VIth form also suggested in 1966 that there should be a new system of authority to replace the prefectorial system. It had always been an aim of the school to encourage pupils to take responsibility. In fact in 1957 there were written into what was known as the Friday Book (used at Lists and Second Hall) as many as 91 offices, including such positions as Scribe, Assistant Scribe, Apprentice Scribe, Dinner Messenger and Bellman. This last one involved watching the clock and leaving each lesson in time to ring the bell by hand. It was a much-coveted office. The VIth form now suggested a sharing out of duties between the whole VIth form, instead of the appointment of Prefects. The system of voting for head-girl and deputy by the form after general discussion of the strengths and weaknesses of every possible candidate was also accepted. Though in some years this produced a head-girl whom staff would not have chosen, some of these unexpected appointments proved remarkably good, and the fact that the VIth form had done the chosing themselves meant, in theory at least, that they were supportive. It was for her encouragement of participation and her welcoming of consultation that Miss Ayre is particularly remembered, as well as for her kindness. Detailed organisation was not her strongest point. She herself joked about her vagueness about things like where she had left her handbag. Miss Porten's efficiency made up for this, and filled in where Miss Ayre was not so strong.

There were two major changes in personnel towards the end of Miss Ayre's time. In 1967 Miss Ann Penny retired as Head of Limes. She was of course its first head, coming back from Somerset to take charge. She was not originally a junior school teacher, but trained in Art. However, in wartime people turned their hands to whatever job was needed. Her mother lived with her in the Limes and her sister Kay taught Speech and

Drama to pupils throughout the school. The tributes that were made at her retirement all talked of the happiness of the Junior department of the school. The development of separate Lists, separate Sports Days and eventually separate timings of lunch breaks was really a response to growing numbers rather than any wish to create a separate school or personal empire, which would have been completely alien to Miss Penny's nature. Her quietness did not preclude a formidable presence and a capacity to sum up and judge. Small girls would like her but not joke with her. She died in October 1996.

The other change, also in 1967, which was received with sadness, was the sudden death of Mabel Waite, who had continued to be a general comforter and help even after the end of boarding. She had been a no-nonsense sort of nanny to generations of house-girls and cared for them and the day-girls when they were ill. She had an uncanny understanding of when the illness was caused by the desire to avoid a lesson! Her comfort in other sorts of trouble was remembered with affection by day-girls and house-girls alike, and her occasional brusqueness forgiven. An award was given in her memory to one pupil each year who was going on to nursing or some related career. This was funded by the Old Crohamians' Association.

By the time Miss Ayre retired in 1970 the new laboratories were in use as well as the Assembly Hall. The VIth-form Basic course was flourishing, the VIth form no longer had to wear uniform and were taking responsibility corporately for duties in the school. The numbers of pupils in the school had risen to 422 (including 14 in VIth General, 21 in the other Lower VIth, 20 in the Upper VIth and 7 in the Third Year VIth), and there was a band of dedicated teachers working happily together. Croham Hurst, however, was no longer a boarding school, one of the things which had distinguished it from other independent girls' schools in the Croydon area. Although it now had a wider curriculum, new facilities and a more academic image, and had weathered the enormous changes in patterns of thought in this period, there were new challenges to face. State education became more of a competitor, and rapid inflation made it more and more difficult for parents to keep up with the inevitable rises in fees.

CHAPTER 4

1970-1986

'Time future contained in time past'

No independent school can flourish in a time of inflation and recession, if there is a viable alternative in state education, unless it has something distinctive to offer. Croham Hurst's beginnings were when there was very little state education for girls. Its distinctiveness in the early years was created by Miss Clark's personality, and by the emphasis on the development of each individual's character, regardless of her academic ability. It was also a boarding school, unlike the larger girls' schools in Croydon such as Croydon High School and Old Palace School. It was the friendly atmosphere, and the social skills of the girls, which persuaded many parents to choose it. By 1970, however, it was no longer a boarding school, so a little of the family atmosphere had gone, and it had become larger and more academic. In 1971 Croydon Education Authority introduced comprehensive education. To begin with, while parents were still doubtful about the change, this worked in favour of the independent girls' schools, but later, as it became a settled and successful system, people who formerly might have sent their daughters to independent schools rather than to Secondary Modern schools now sent them to the state comprehensive schools. Since Old Palace and Croydon High, choosing to retain selective entry, had now to lose the Local Authority free places for 50 per cent of their pupils, it meant that there were now more available paying places in independent girls' schools in Croydon. Also, as boys' public schools started to take girls in the VIth form, and as Sixth Form Colleges developed, there were further problems for a small girls' school.

The new headmistress of Croham Hurst, Doreen Seward, was aware that the job was a challenge. There were aspects of the school she particularly wished to cherish—the atmosphere, the unusual nature of the buildings, the traditions (like cornflowers on Old Crohamians' Day), the great loyalty of the old-girls, the high moral stance of a school with Quaker beginnings, the interest in each individual girl. But there were also things which, in spite of the rapid changes of the previous 20 years, she felt needed changing further, particularly in the facilities and the widening of the curriculum, if Croham Hurst were to maintain its position in an increasingly competitive world.

Miss Seward had a wider and more varied experience than previous headmistresses. She had, as a child, wanted to be a dancer. After her schooldays at the North London Collegiate school, she trained in Physical Education, getting a London University Diploma in P.E. Later, she acquired an Honours degree in history from London University, and also a Diploma in Theology. As she herself put it, this showed her interest in the whole person, body, mind and spirit. She had taught at Watford Grammar School, and her old school of North London Collegiate, had lectured at Stockwell College of Education, and had been Second Head (that is, Senior Mistress) at Sutton High School, G.P.D.S.T. She was always a keen gardener and after her retirement she became a keen painter. In fact she was a person with many interests, suitable for a school whose

63 *Miss Seward*

distinguishing aim was emphasis on the development of the whole personality. Her 16 years at the school saw many changes, many stresses, and it was not clear in these years what direction education was going to take in the country at large.

Miss Seward was a meticulous, careful and conscientious head, respected by parents and pupils alike. She was aware of what was going on in each department of the school. She personally looked at the content of all exams., for instance, and took the decisions about the ordering of text books, expeditions and other details. She dealt personally with discipline problems, career options, and the minutiae of school life. It was a tight ship she ran and, as its captain and figure-head, she maintained a controlled, immaculately dressed, one could almost say regal, persona. She was frequently to be seen walking round the school, always with poise and dignity, and always aware of what was going on. A gentle sense of humour lightened this style of leadership. Miss Seward was concerned for staff, pupils and parents as individuals, and took great pains to help those who went to her with personal problems, showing a personal concern which continued after retirement. She remained firmly at the helm for 16 years, but then decided to retire a few years early to allow her successor both to introduce and carry through the impending government-imposed changes. On her retirement the Old Crohamians surprised her with a 'This is your life' programme which gave them the opportunity to show her the affection they had for her.

In 1970 Miss Seward arrived full of energy and enthusiasm. She is reported as saying she was 'absolutely sold on the school'. The architecture of the original school intrigued her, and she resisted suggestions for alterations to the original hall by lowering the ceiling, or to the original drawing room by splitting it into two. (In fact the Small Hall is still substantially the same as it appears in the photograph of 1907!) Some things Miss Seward changed at the outset, like the tradition by which girls who had been in trouble the previous week stood up in Assembly and announced what they had done wrong. This custom might have had its origin in the idea of repentance, but it had become a ceremony which glorified the 'crimes'. She also, soon after her arrival, changed the school song, feeling that Cecily Mackray's composition was somewhat dated. At Assembly she introduced a short time of silence, in keeping with the Quaker traditions of the school. Miss Seward was not a Quaker, though her Christian faith was her deepest motivation and she regarded the daily Assembly as extremely important. For some years the talk she gave at the first Assembly of term was a moral drawn from some sheep she had seen on her holidays. The VIth-form leavers in 1978 gave Miss Seward a toy sheep, as a joke. It was treasured by her in the drawing room.

As always, many of the changes in the school were driven, not by the headmistress's personal ideals, but by changes outside. During Miss Seward's time at Croham Hurst there were considerable changes in educational thinking, resulting in changed examination syllabuses. By now there were wider options at universities, with combinations of subjects and joint degrees becoming popular. It is much easier for a large school to offer a wide range of subjects; small schools find it difficult to finance this. It was obvious to Miss Seward that, if Croham Hurst were to offer a full range of science teaching, and the possibility of choosing A-levels from both arts and sciences, and also the newer subjects like economics, it would have to expand even further, so that there would be a large enough VIth form and a large enough staff to make possible the complicated time-tabling necessary for wide options. The science labs had been seen to be too small almost as soon as they had been built, now that Physics, Chemistry and Biology were taught separately at A-level and throughout the school. The senior school was already two-stream by 1965, but Miss Seward felt it needed to be larger, and in 1974 she took in a third stream, intending to do this every five years, as well as making the Limes two-stream throughout. This eventually meant that the VIth form increased to 68 by 1986, though it later receded a little, in spite of the larger intake, because of the growing popularity of Sixth Form Colleges. In 1970 there were 429 on the school roll; by 1986 there were 596.

64 *Miss Seward with the VIth form*

65 *The VIth form common-room*

66 *The Garden Wing with the cherry tree*

This expansion was of course made possible only by further building. The first improvement was the re-arrangement of the VIth-form facilities. For a time the Upper and Lower VIth shared a common-room, until they became too large. Mrs. Bywater had died in 1968, and gifts given in her memory by old-girls were used towards the equipment of a separate VIth-form library. The first major project was the building of three new class-rooms, rather grandly known as the Garden Wing, in 1973. Fortunately, the beautiful cherry tree was kept, but by now no one could describe the school, as Miss Wickham had done, as 'in a pleasant garden'. Very little of the original garden was now left. Another development was the changing of the workshop and the sickroom. In 1977 the Jubilee Wing was completed. This was a two-storey extension to the existing science block, allowing for an A-level biology lab. at the ground-floor level, and a Textiles and Craft room above. Fine Art was transferred to the Vineyard, making possible a VIth-form common-room in the attic of the Middle House. In 1979 the loft in the Vineyard was converted to a studio, expanding the facilities for art. In 1981 the Limes had a beautiful new gym which could be used for the Carol Service and other large assemblies, and in 1983 the old lean-to lavatories in the Limes, a legacy of its days as a boys' prep school, were replaced with a proper block.

The largest building project undertaken was the new Gym and Music Centre for the senior school, known as the Doreen Seward Centre, with a very original music room named after Derek Rogers. He had been Chairman of the governors from 1974 to 1978 and had died of cancer in February 1984. Music had been his main joy, though his professional expertise, which he put at the service of the school, was in merchant banking, as Director of J. Henry Schroder Wagg and Co. After his death, his wife and daughter Wendy gave a music prize in his memory. The new gym was named after Ellinor Hinks, who had been a pupil at the school in Miss Clark's day, had gone on to become Principal of Nonington Physical Education College, the first women's P.E. College to take men,

67 *The Doreen Seward Centre*

and was the chairman of Croham Hurst's governors from 1978 to 1985. She had made films of gym and dance which are used round the world, and designed apparatus to cater for modern trends in the study of movement, which the school has used. This building was such an expense that advice on fund-raising was put in the hands of professional fund-raisers. The cost of the scheme was £220,000. Hundreds of personal letters were written to those connected with the school. The expertise of the Finance Committee of the governors was such that all these building developments were achieved without the

68 *Ellinor Hinks with Dame Ninette de Valois, Miss Seward and Wing Commander Buckland, the Bursar, at Speech Day 1979*

school ever going into debt. Miss Seward's delight at the completion of the project was such that she fulfilled her promise to the chairman of the fund-raising committee, Colin Hart, and danced a polka across the gym floor.

The largest project for building had actually come to nothing. Negotiations had started sometime around 1970 for closer links with Whitgift School, mooted it would appear, by Mr. Marten, an Old Whitgiftian, a governor of Croham Hurst, husband and father of Old Crohamians and by then Chairman of the Whitgift Foundation. The plan put forward in 1975 was for a merger of Whitgift and Croham Hurst, including the building of a completely new school on Croham Hurst golf course, with boys up to 16 in one building, girls up to 16 in another, and a joint VIth-form centre linking the two. This would, of course, have solved all Croham Hurst's problems about purpose-built facilities, and would have provided a big enough VIth form and staff to allow very wide combinations of subjects. However, it might have been at the cost of much that made Croham Hurst what it was, the distinctive emphasis and traditions. Local residents objected very strongly to the loss of the golf course and, while protracted negotiations went on about planning permission, inflation roared away, and made the cost of such a project prohibitive. So Croham Hurst lost the security that the endowments of the Whitgift Foundation would have given it, but retained its own identity and distinctiveness. Fortunately Whitgift and Croham Hurst continued to maintain links. Girls from Croham Hurst became involved in Whitgift productions during these years, and were invited to VIth-form lectures, while at one stage Whitgift boys joined Croham Hurst's cookery classes.

In his speech at the opening of the Wagstaff Library, Mr. Patterson, Chairman of the governors, had said of Croham Hurst, 'the school became widely known, not only for the quality and soundness of its education, but also for the character of its old girls'. Sir William Hamilton Fyfe had said in 1954, 'It is too much to say that you can always tell an Old Cro., but there is something about them which is due to the tone, the tradition, the character of the school'. In 1958 Miss Wickham said, 'The true worth of any school is finally determined by the mettle of its past pupils'. At Speech Day in 1957 Mr. Jennings, a housemaster at Marlborough, told the staff that the test of their work was what their pupils would be like at forty. These quotations come from the 1950s, but it is true that many of the features of the school in the '70s and '80s can also be best illustrated by the subsequent lives of some of the pupils of this time.

69 *Catriona Boulton*

Catriona Boulton (now Forrest), one of the many relatives of Hazel Inglis who had passed through the school, was one of the girls who benefited from the wider choice which the new buildings made possible. Trina became an architect, training at Bath University and the Polytechnic of Central London where she got her RIBA in 1981. She wanted to take Maths,

Physics, History and Art at A-level, excellent subjects to support Architecture. Not many women were reading Architecture yet. In a small school it is more practical to divide the VIth form into arts or sciences and timetable these groups of subjects against each other. In simpler days, when Miss Porten did the timetable, that was how it worked. Now Miss Seward herself did the timetable, in co-operation with Ruth Barclay, Head of Science, and after 1981 with Rosemary Porter. The weeks of timetabling in the summer term were a tense time at the drawing room end of the school, but Trina's preferences were accommodated and an architect she became. She worked on several historic building and restoration projects, the most recent of which was the restoration of 16 Carlton House Terrace for the Crown Commissioners. She particularly enjoyed the research phase, for which the subjects she was able to study at school were specially useful.

70 *Carole Dodd*

Carole Dodd (now Nicholson) was another pupil who in the early '70s had set her heart on mixing arts and sciences, taking Latin, Maths and Physics. The school's timetable was arranged in the first instance round the VIth-form choices and then the O-level options, and the assumption in 1973 had been that Carole would do Maths, Physics and Biology. It had to be completely re-thought to allow her to take Latin. Carole was, at the time of writing, Group Treasurer and Director of a large multi-national property company, the only woman on the board. The advantage of being in a small school where you knew everyone, and where all the VIth form took responsibilities in the school, had helped her, she believed, in pursuing her chosen path through accountancy training. She chose to work with companies which structured their teams into divisions of about thirty people, a size of group Carole was comfortable with after her experience at Croham Hurst. Both Trina and Carole, who succeeded in slightly unusual fields, felt the advantages of a school small enough to have a family feel and yet able, because of Miss Seward's efforts, to be flexible enough to allow unusual choices.

Arranging the staffing far enough in advance and avoiding classes too small to be economic when in some years only one or two pupils opted for, say, A-level Music, were other problems for timetabling. As universities offered more joint courses, and additional subjects had to be included, it became even more complicated. At A-level, Food and Nutrition, Religious Studies, Government and Politics, Textiles and Economics were added to the possible choices. For those staying only one year in the VIth form, Computer Studies and Human Biology at O-level were made available. Lower down the school, the timetable had to include Health Education, Careers and three separate sciences. To complicate it further, C.S.E.s were introduced in the 4th year in certain subjects for girls who found O-levels too demanding. In 1974 a completely different timetable of a less academic nature was run concurrently with the normal one for a very small group of girls. Back in 1946, the 4th-year curriculum had consisted merely of History, Geography, English, Latin, Art, Algebra and General Science. By the 1980s there had to be a complicated system of 'blocks' of subjects from which choices could be made. For example, Block 1 could be Biology or Human Biology, 2: Chemistry or Geography or Art, 3: Physics or Physics with Chemistry or Cookery, 4: German or Geography or CSE History, 5: Latin or Music or Social Studies or Cookery, 6: History or Religious Studies. To this were added the compulsory subjects of English, Maths, French and PE and Games. This is difficult to read. It was difficult to make the choices. It was difficult to timetable. It was small wonder that the weeks of timetabling became a dreaded period.

Sadaf Ghaem Maghami illustrates another development of these years. She came to England with her parents in 1983 from Iran. She had very little English, but was determined to be a doctor, although her language did not appear to be adequate to study science A-levels. With her determination, with intensive coaching in English from Sheila Koeze (an Old Crohamian who had returned to CHS), with help from Miss Seward and other staff in making applications, Sadaf achieved her ambition and became a doctor at the London Hospital and then undertook research in gynaecology. Her story reminds us that in the '60s, '70s and '80s there were large numbers of immigrants into England, some from Britain's former colonies, some from countries where there were violent changes, some coming as businessmen for a short term. *The Crohamian* of 1973 describes school days in other cultures previously experienced by girls in the school that year. Mentioned were Austria, Burma, Canada, Cyprus, Germany, Greece, India, Iran, Japan, Libya, Malta, Spain, Uganda, USA and Vietnam! This meant, of course, a larger proportion of girls from faiths other than Christianity, and some who came with very little English.

The school's stated aim was to enable each individual to achieve her own potential. Back in 1956 the governors had authorised Miss Wickham to take a part-time teacher in the Limes to help those who had special difficulties with English and Maths. Now special provision was made in the senior school for those with language difficulties or other learning difficulties like dyslexia. Mrs. Lansdowne, mother of a pupil, was one of the first to provide this. Mrs. Cheeseman, mother of a former pupil, who had taught English and Languages, and coached girls needing Latin for university, now concentrated on helping those learning English as a second (or in some cases third or fourth) language, and developed a particular rapport with her Japanese pupils. Sheila Koeze added to her other skills a special training in teaching those with dyslexia, as did Judith Ellingham, encouraged by Miss Seward. It was astonishing how quickly most of those arriving with little or no English, like Sadaf, or with dyslexia or other learning difficulties, were able to take a full part in the life of the school.

The '70s and '80s were years in which society as a whole became both conscious and concerned about the disadvantages women had in their careers. It now became easier for women to choose the career that suited them, instead of being guided into traditional women's careers. A surprising number of early Crohamians had become doctors, dentists and scientific researchers; surprising since the facilities for science were so lacking in the school till the 1960s. But most girls had done the obvious teaching or nursing training and then married. Those who distinguished themselves tended to be in the artistic field, like Margaret Pilkington in the Whitworth Art Gallery (she left the school before 1910),

Sheila Macqueen, who, as Sheila Young, was in the school in the 1920s and became famous as a flower arranger, or Barbara Batt (who left in 1925) a maker of stained glass windows. Andrée Wellstead (1953) was another artist. She fulfilled her childhood ambition to be like Oliver Messel, and became a designer for the theatre and for television, including such well-known programmes as 'Jackanory', 'Omnibus' and 'Yes, Minister'. Even Robin Hammond (1933) who became a lecturer at New Hall, Cambridge, did so in the well-loved discipline of English, and of course as a teacher, though at a very high level. Now careers became more diverse.

Miss Wickham had given Miss Porten special responsibility for careers, but she was also Second Mistress and was in charge of timetabling. Now a teacher was actually given timetabled time for careers—first Mrs. Plumstead and then Mrs. Payne. In 1981 a proper careers library was made in memory of Miss Balcombe who had died in the previous year at the age of 96, ending 52 years of association with the school. As she had always kept in such close contact with Old Crohamians, remembering and following their careers, and had given the Honours board to the school, facilities for careers advice seemed a fitting memorial to her.

In the '60s and '70s it had been possible to take advantage of Local Authority careers advice, and Mr. Evernden, the Youth Employment Officer of the Croydon Borough Careers Service, would come to the school. When independent schools were denied local authority help, the school joined the Independent Schools' Careers Organisation, though later the local authority provision was restored. In addition to lectures and interviews, the school held their first Careers Evening in 1980, and subsequently a Careers Convention became a yearly event, with parents and companies agreeing to set up stalls to answer questions. The school also benefited from having on its governing body for a time Miss Hilton, who had been Organising Secretary of the National Advisory Centre on Careers for Women, and was a world authority on careers for women.

Work experience for the Vth and VIth forms was another innovation to encourage an informed choice of career. Inevitably more pupils continued to choose teaching, nursing and other caring careers, rather than business careers. Perhaps the continuing encouragement to the VIth form to help at the Limes or at Rutherford, the centre for sufferers from cerebral palsy in Melville Avenue, played a part in this. But business in a very limited way did actually enter the school premises in 1982, in the form of the Young Enterprise scheme. VIth formers could be seen rushing around school trying to sell hand-made earrings, or fluffy animals to fit on the top of pencils. The scheme was intended to encourage the VIth form to understand what was involved in running a business. With help from Nestlé, teams had to be formed to run a company. A managing director, company secretary and other officers had to be chosen, capital had to be raised, a product had to be invented and marketed and the profit, if any, had to be distributed to the shareholders. Not many Crohamians have become managing directors as a result, but understanding of the business world was increased.

Some larger schools might have provided more careers advice and might have better facilities than Croham Hurst, whose teachers were too involved in their subject teaching to be able to get much first-hand knowledge of the world of outside work. However, Elissa Sabine was one of many at Croham Hurst who felt that personal encouragement

71 *Elissa Sabine*

given and personal confidence engendered was more important than the actual knowledge and information available. Elissa became the school's first electronics engineer in 1982, having got a first-class degree in this subject. She went on to work on advanced, complex systems for BT's Research Laboratories, and then set up her own consultancy company. Elissa was an all-rounder at school and could have done well in any chosen field. She was regarded as a bit of a pioneer in choosing electronics, as a woman. In 1988 still only four per cent of professional engineers and scientists were women. There were other unusual choices at this time. Elizabeth Dailey got a degree in building-surveying, and Karen McRobert was encouraged to train in agriculture though many felt this was not a suitable career for women. More Crohamians went on to study law. But it is still true that many of these trail-blazers, Elissa and Trina among them, later put their careers on hold in order to bring up children. This is a good reason for a girls' school to emphasise more than just academic prowess.

It was to be expected that with her own training in Physical Education Miss Seward should want to encourage it at Croham Hurst. A small day school for girls, however, is never likely to achieve great success in sport, measured by the winning of trophies, though the remembered enjoyment of the pupils is a form of success open to any school. Lacrosse, which remained Croham Hurst's most important sport since the 1921 referendum, is anyway a minority game. Netball and tennis were also played, and rounders, but of course larger schools tended to win the competitions for these. Dance was also an important element in the P.E. at Croham Hurst, remembered by pupils of the '20s and '30s as Greek dancing, for which they wore shapeless tunics. In the years when Frances Press (Waller) was teaching there were some spectacular dance productions, *Alice* and *Jesus Christ Superstar* in particular. Elizabeth Cheyne, who taught at the school from 1972-9, also gave a lot of emphasis to individual expression in modern dance. But this is not competitive and its success cannot be measured. The actual standard achieved obviously depends on the talents of the pupils at any given time. In competitive sports, Croham Hurst's success was variable! 1972 was one of the years the school did well in the All England Schools' Lacrosse Tournament, only to be followed in 1974 by a season in which the school team lost all the games it played.

From 1976, however, for several years the school did achieve measurable success. Fiona Craig (now Simpson), who was at school at that time, is one of several Crohamians who played lacrosse at county and national level. She claimed that she found her inspiration largely in two successive teachers at the school, Sandi Procter and Judy Gorrie, who themselves were playing for England. They gave up much of their spare time to take Fiona, and others like her, Julia Whyke, Sally Goodliffe and Joanne Russell among them, to the Centre of Excellence for Lacrosse on Monday evenings and to organise early morning

practices at school. Fiona remembered often going to watch them
play in matches, and being inspired
by their play, and wishing to please
them. In 1978 and 1981 the school
lacrosse teams were taken on a visit
to the U.S.A. where they won every
match they played. Fiona was in
the England Junior side in 1981
and in the England team in 1982
and for some years after she left
school. She has continued playing
lacrosse for pleasure in such time
as she could spare from teaching,
or looking after her young son. So
the love of the sport she acquired

72 *Julia Whyke, Karen Carter-Pegg, Sarah Lawrence and Fiona Craig when members of the Surrey 1st Lacrosse team*

at school is being handed on to the next generation. Fiona was happy at Croham Hurst,
where she absorbed the attitude that playing well and achieving her own potential was
more important than winning a league table. Fiona is only one of many who learnt to
love sport, and of several who rose to the top. In 1991, for instance, there were three
Crohamians playing for Wales: Karen Owen (Carter-Pegg), Sarah Lawrence and Vicky
Oakley. Possibly some of the high-fliers might feel that they would have been stretched
further in a larger school, but perhaps they would have been less encouraged.

When Old Crohamians of whatever period are asked what were the highlights of
their time at school, they almost always mention some dramatic production. These had
been a feature of Croham Hurst's life since the early days, when Miss Clark herself wrote
many of the plays performed, like 'Croham Hurst and the Postman', or 'Some Dreams
Come True'. 'The Treasure of Reydonar' was highly thought of at the time and was
published. It would not be easy to put on today, containing as it does lines like: 'But, great
heaven, it is a preposterous business'. 'Some Dreams Come True' was in verse, and must
have been difficult to memorise. One speech ran:

> Why this is scorn!
> And scorn may never light the temple torch
> At wisdom's altar. Nay, the outer porch
> Is quite denied presumptuous votaries.

But pupils of Miss Clark's days loved her plays. Obviously the standards of productions, of whatever period, depended not only on the abilities of the pupils, but even more
on the availability of a member of staff with gifts for producing. But whatever the
standard, the effect on girls taking part seems to have been immense. Some productions
which seem to have been regarded as remarkable were *The Zeal of Thy House* produced
by Miss Miller in 1954, and *Romeo and Juliet* produced by Jane Buckingham, with Lindsay
Kemp and Gillian Baldwin in the lead roles. This was in 1958 and was the school's first
full-scale Shakespearean production. Also remembered as spectacular were the *Medieval*

73 Romeo and Juliet

Mysteries in 1961 and *Victoriana* in 1963, both produced by Elizabeth Rumbelow and both involving lots of girls and lots of skills, and also the dance production of *Alice* by Frances Press(Waller) in 1967.

In the 1980s, however, the productions seem to have become more professional. There are various possible reasons for this. One was the arrival on the scene in 1981 of Mr. and Mrs. Flook to help with the lighting. They had done this for various other schools and dramatic societies in the area, and they had considerable expertise both in the technical and artistic aspects and also in teaching the pupils how to do lighting for plays. They were also generous with their own equipment. Even plays with really difficult challenges, for which the school's lighting facilities were not adequate, were to them just another interesting problem to be solved. These included *Lark Rise* in 1983, which was done in the round, and *The Dragon* in 1993 which used a combination of recorded and direct speech and various special effects. Another factor contributing to the extra polish of the productions was the experience gained by Whitgift's invitation to some Croham Hurst girls to share in some of their productions, such as the joint production of *Much Ado About Nothing* in 1983. Whitgift had many resources at its disposal, and even took some productions on tour to Germany. Croham Hurst benefited from this and obviously acting with people of the opposite sex also added a new dimension!

If the test of a school is what the pupils are doing in the later years, then the '80s were vintage years for drama. There had been former Crohamians who had become professional actresses. Sheila Grant (1945-51), whose family owned what was then Croydon's major department store, acted often on radio, and appeared on stage and television, in 'Bergerac' and 'The Bill' among other well-known series. Sally Adams (1951-6) who joined the Mermaid Theatre Company, and Ann Merry, Secretary of the newly formed Dramatic Society at the school in 1954, also became professional actresses. There were, however, several pupils from the 1980s who at the time of writing were working professionally in the theatre and television and radio. Sara Markland appeared as a professional in *Annie* and *The Secret Garden* while she was still a pupil. She left school before

74 *Sara Markland*

completing her A-levels, to appear in the lead role of Pandora in *The Secret Diary of Adrian Mole*, on the West End stage. She has subsequently done work on television, in radio and on the stage, in the West End and in other parts of Britain and in America, and in 1997 she joined the Royal Shakespeare Company. She felt the encouragement to act professionally and yet not neglect her school work was an important influence on her. Susan Perkins became the first woman President of the famous Cambridge Foot-lights, and as a comedienne and writer has worked for several well-known radio and television shows as well as leading educational tours. In 1997 she and her co-writer had their own programme on Channel 4, 'Light Lunch', said by *The Daily Telegraph* to be a 'surprise hit'. Her debt to the school was partly the encouragement she received to talk, and the accept-ance of individuality, which Susan unmistakeably had.

Heidi Porter, after some time as a dancer, joined the 'Circle in the Square' performing arts group in New York. Sally Spurring, another pupil from these years, was working in radio, and Sarah Branston, who took the lead in school plays a few years later, not only taught English and Drama but was also acting professionally at the time of writing. Joanne Bradman got a taste for stage management which was powerfully reinforced at college, and eventually gave up her 'safe' career to work as assistant stage manager on various West End productions.

All these girls mentioned the same ways in which the school had influenced their subsequent development. One way was that in a small school they could at an early age experience the excitement of being involved in school productions—a sentiment echoed by Mabel Weiss from the early days under Miss Clark. The teaching of Speech and Drama as an optional extra went back many years also. Miss Kay Penny (sister of Ann who was Head of the Junior department until 1967) had taught it in the Limes Annexe, commonly known as the hut. It was she who gave the Kay Penny trophy for Speech and Drama, which is a rose bowl exactly the same age as the school. After her retirement the torch was carried on by Carol Schroeder, whom this group of girls remember with gratitude, for her lessons, her productions, and her encouragement to enter festivals. There were opportunities not only to act but to produce and to train others. From the early days the house-girls had written and acted plays in their 'sets' at weekends. When Miss Wickham introduced Houses, a House Drama competition was begun. The years 1979–82 saw the expansion of this into an Eisteddfod including music, dance, art and craft, creative writing and even computer programming as well as drama. The organisation of this required an exercise in co-operation and the interaction of the arts.

The main school productions of the '80s were ambitious, and this group of girls, Sara, Susan, Sarah and others who have not made the theatre their career, look back with gratitude to two members of staff in particular who challenged them to do far more than

75 The Magic Flute

they had imagined possible: Lorraine Gwynne and Stephen Adams. First came a performance of *Dido and Aeneas* in 1982. In 1983 came the elaborate performance of *Lark Rise*.
In 1984 there was a joint production with Whitgift School of the musical *Drake* which
went on to the Edinburgh Festival. They then got involved in the Children's Music
Theatre, and performed at the Young Vic. The year 1985 saw the production of the *Magic
Flute*. For a small girls' school this was a wildly ambitious project, but one which, for those
who took part, expanded their ideas of the achievable. They visited the Royal Opera
House, and members of the Royal Opera House were persuaded by Mrs. Gwynne to help
in getting the production off the ground. Miss Clark would have approved. One of her
chosen mottoes was: 'He shoots higher far who aims the sky, than he who aims a tree'.
The girls who took part are shooting higher still. Mr. Raeburn, Headmaster of Whitgift,
said afterwards:

> The performance showed how much can be achieved thro' clear, true, beau-
> tifully phrased singing by girls who were clearly inspired by Mozart, and had
> worked hard enough to be able to communicate their feeling for him in a truly
> effortless way. Mrs. Gwynne offered her pupils something great, and they re-
> sponded to her challenge. What more can a teacher ask and achieve?

1985 must have been a rather special year, according to *The Crohamian*. In sport in this year the first lacrosse team did well in the Surrey Tournament. For the first time girls from the school joined the Cross-Country Championship and the senior team came first. One girl, Caroline Letchford, came first in the county. Three girls represented Croydon at the Surrey Schools' Championship. There was a ski-ing trip, and a visit of a lacrosse team from Garrison First School, Baltimore. Theatre visits included two different performances of *Measure for Measure*, *As You Like It* at the RSC, Tom Stoppard's *Jumpers*, *Daisy Pulls It Off*, *Of Mice and Men* at the Mermaid, *Cider with Rosie*, *Hamlet* at the Young Vic, and another performance of *Hamlet* and of *Richard III* on the annual visit to Stratford-on-Avon. Geography expeditions included the VIth form to Cuckmere Haven, the Lower Vth to Mole River Valley, the Upper IVth to the Commonwealth Institute, the Lower IVth to Bewl Reservoir and the Upper IIIrd to the Geology Museum. There was a German exchange and a French Cookery trip, and several visits to French films and plays. Musical visits included a Christmas Concert when girls met the London Symphony Orchestra, a backstage visit at the Royal Opera House before the ballet of Cinderella, a song masterclass by Ian Partridge at Trinity College Cambridge, a visit to Finchcocks, a Haydn Study Weekend with Professor Robbins-Landon, a Mendelssohn Concerto at St John's,

76 *Loraine Gwynne and the choir in Bourges Cathedral*

Smith Square, visits to *42nd Street* and *West Side Story*, to the Monteverdi Choir singing Bach's B-minor Mass at the Queen Elizabeth Hall, and to a Schubert Song Cycle by Hermann Prey. Some girls attended holiday music courses, and toured Holland with the Youth Orchestra. There were lunchtime concerts given in school by Mary Morley and Nicholas Roberts, and of course the usual school concerts and musical items at Speech Day and the Christmas Carol Service and Founders' Day. In Art, visits were made to the Thyssen-Bornemisza Collection at the Royal Academy, the Renoir Exhibition at the Hayward Gallery, Edward Lear's paintings at the Tate, and also an Exhibition of GCSE Art and Design work and the Cadbury Exhibition of Children's Art. Many of these things were done regularly, but no other year seems to have had quite as many expeditions as 1985 did. One almost wonders where the ordinary work of the curriculum was fitted in! Miss Clark's motto, 'Life is not a closed door but an open road', might have been a suitable motto for this year.

The '60s had seen an increase in freedom of expression and the development of a specific youth culture. This led to much questioning of authority, which made it difficult to maintain discipline in any school. Attitudes to school uniform in the '70s were just one example of this. In Croham Hurst it became impossible to enforce the wearing of hats.

There were frequent suggestions for the alteration of school uniform to make it more contemporary—a difficult exercise, as fashion changed so rapidly. The VIth form eventually won their battle to be allowed to wear jeans in school (they had ceased to wear uniform in 1969). Old rules like silence in the corridors went. VIth formers were permitted to go home early on afternoons when they were not timetabled for lessons. Pupils no longer leapt to their feet when staff approached. No one wanted the abandonment of good manners, but society's estimate of what counted as good manners had changed.

Maintaining order but allowing freedom is a difficult exercise, particularly when prevailing habits of thought question authority more and more. That it was achieved in Croham Hurst was partly due to the care taken by Miss Seward, and partly to the efforts of the super-efficient second mistress from 1971 to 1981, Margery Mellor. As the school grew it became more complicated to provide cover for absent staff and to arrange rooms (particularly after the change to teaching in subject rooms rather than form rooms). The overseeing of examinations, dealing with the innumerable petty problems of discipline which arise in any school, and the day-to-day management of the staff were other tasks which escalated with the school's size. Mrs. Mellor's schedules and lists were always perfect, and she seemed never to make a mistake. In exercising discipline—and no-one crossed Mrs. Mellor lightly—she had sympathy with the merely non-conformist whose deviations were not malicious, and a belief in the importance of individual freedom. She held the staff together as a group, partly by the exercise of generous hospitality, in spite of the increasing numbers and the division of the teaching space into subject-related areas.

One response to demands for greater freedom is to grant greater responsibility. The school magazine had started as a production for Old Crohamians, edited by Miss Lyall from 1914, and then by Miss Wickham herself and Miss Balcombe. The first articles were written by old-girls for old-girls and the only contributions from the school were the head's articles and the anonymous poems written in the Book of Honour. By 1938 there were a few poems and accounts of holidays from the girls, and by 1956 there was a complete school section. The original cover design by Margaret Pilkington was changed in 1960 to feature the Coat of Arms. This year the practice of listing all the old-girls was discontinued. But in 1969 the magazine was changed again. It was Miss Vincent's idea to produce the magazine photographically, making it possible to have a much more imaginative layout and to include far more illustrations. (Pauline Vincent was the head of the Art department.) In the '70s and '80s the magazine was largely written by the pupils, with pupil editors and photos of individuals and jokey accounts of VIth-form aspirations or comments made by Terence, a strange cartoon dog. Staff editors, like Linda Wilkinson, continued however to have a very important role in encouragement and co-ordination.

Greater participation in the magazine was one change. Another was the introduction by Miss Seward of participation by pupils in the Head's Report on Speech Day, an innovation universally appreciated. The School Council, started in Miss Ayre's time, also assumed more importance, though it was still only a suggestions forum. A lot of its time was spent discussing irksome minor school rules, and rules about school uniform—Could the socks be blue? Could the blouses have short sleeves? Might leg-warmers be worn in winter? Could burgundy-coloured shoes be added to the permitted black or brown? But some real decisions were taken. A questionnaire on the school hymn was arranged and a referendum on whether to keep school houses (they were kept). Progress prizes, form prayers, being allowed to stay in the school building at Rest and the introduction of Mufti Day (when girls are allowed to wear non-uniform clothes in return for a donation to charity) were all suggestions of the School Council. VIth formers were also now involved in discussing their own progress at Parents' Evenings, instead of their parents and teachers discussing them over their heads, or behind their backs as it seemed to some of them.

Not only pupils, but also parents now wanted more say in what was done. Miss Wickham had attempted to replace the Exhibition with its emphasis on 'occupations' and on art, drama and dancing, with an Open Day when parents could attend lessons and see other aspects of the work done. The experiment had been abandoned for lack of space, but Miss Seward attempted it again in 1970. Of course a day-time opening excluded many fathers, so in 1974 it became an Open Evening. Art and music still figured largely, but the academic work of the school was also on display. Prospective parents started to come as well as existing ones, so in 1980 a separate evening for them was arranged, with more chance for consultation.

The concern of parents to be involved in the school was regularised by the forma-tion of the Parents' Guild in 1976 'to encourage and extend co-operation between parents past and present with the school by engaging in cultural, social, educational and possibly sporting activities'. The Parents' Guild has provided a great deal of help to the school. In addition to social functions, like a Victorian Evening, Barn Dance, Fashion Show or Supper Shuffle, each year they organised a Garden Party. With the proceeds they have provided the school over the years with many gifts, such as the first colour television for the Limes, a baby grand piano for the new Music Room, and equipment for the Textile and Design Studio.

77 *The Parents' Guild Garden Party*

Miss Seward was particularly pleased to be the Head of the Limes as well as the senior school, and like other heads of Croham Hurst made a point of spending one morning a week there if possible. She was always thinking of ways of improving the facilities there, making alterations to classrooms. The fact that pupils started at Limes as young as four and a half added to the family feel of the school. The existence of a junior department should also mean continuity in methods and the easier acceptance of values and standards of behaviour. Certainly the Limes was a happy place. The links with other departments of the school were not, however, easily made, as the different building, separated by the playing field, and the different timings necessitated by the sharing of the Hall for dinner, and the different staff, made for distinctions. As the senior school became more academic, Miss Seward no longer felt able to guarantee a place in it for all Limes girls, since not all of them could happily cope with the curriculum which had been adopted. But no system of judging is infallible, and suggestions that girls might be happier elsewhere were sometimes seen as unfair.

78 *Miss Meadows planting a tree with the Limes girls*

The head of the junior department in Limes throughout Miss Seward's time, and indeed before and after also, was Peggy Meadows. She had joined the school when it was still a boarding school, and had lived in. She took over the leadership of the Limes when Miss Penny retired, and continued the same traditions of a gentle, happy place. She would try new methods to see which worked best, but would not slavishly follow fashions in teaching. She accepted changes like the introduction of computers. She held the staff together and her leadership could be described as a triumph of commonsense.

Each year the Limes had expeditions. Favourites were the Museum of London and Horniman's Museum and Miss Green's visit with the Lower IIIrds to Brighton. The routine continued with harvest festival, a toy service, a carol service, a nativity play. In 1979 the Limes had a visit from the Mayor and Mayoress. This was the year of the junior school production of *The Plotters of Cabbage Patch Corner*, which had been such an inspiration to Sara Markland. There was a book fair, a recording by the Lower IIIrd for the BBC Schools' Service, a visit to the ballet, to Addington Church and to a film on the Tower of London. They also had a visit from a road safety officer and saw a police film. This sort of activity went on year after year, but the staff never seemed to lose the pleasure of laying the foundations for later development. Many stayed for long periods, as in the senior school; the longest serving being Miss Meadows herself, who was there for 41 years, and Brenda Green who did 37 years, many of these as Miss Meadows' deputy. Miss Meadows was appointed in Miss Humphrey's time and Brenda Green started under Miss Wickham and both went on until the 1990s.

79 *A classroom in the Limes in 1969*

Perhaps the most widely known Old Crohamian from this period is Belinda Harley, who hit the national press in a big way when she became for three years Private Secretary to H.R.H. the Prince of Wales, with particular responsibility for arts, heritage and health matters, at a time when royal affairs were hot news. She was the first woman to hold this sort of position in the Prince's household. Belinda was already well known as an organiser of, and publicist for, arts events, running her own public relations company. She was responsible for the well-received Japan Festival at the Victoria and Albert Museum. She had done work for the Prince's Trust and had organised his 40th birthday party in a tram-shed! At the time of writing she was also a governor of the Royal Shakespeare Company, on the publications committee of the Royal Collection, on the Development Council of the British Museum, and Literary Editor of the *Daily Express*. Belinda came to school in the Limes and, in spite of not being a conformist in temperament, found that Croham Hurst gave her sympathy and emotional support when she needed it. She found the discipline, which she describes as a gentle discouragement of bullying, and the tone—'a sort of laid-back Christianity'—strangely congenial. At VIth-form level, the conscious effort to treat pupils as adults, which was not as common in 1970 as it is now, meant that 'we still misbehaved, but felt guilty about it, which is probably as good as you can get'. Individual members of staff, who went beyond the call of duty, are remembered with affection, in particular Miss Rowlatt, who made her free of the book cupboard, and who

80 *Belinda Harley*

with Mrs Mellor, stayed in school after hours to coach her for Oxford entrance. Belinda also spoke warmly of Miss Vincent, for whom no trouble was too much to encourage an appreciation of art, and Ann Currie who arranged lectures on philosophy at Belinda's request and instilled a love of Latin poetry. Although her parents had not envisaged a university career for her, the school encouraged Belinda to aim for Oxford, and she read English at St. Hugh's. So in addition to being an example of the care for and acceptance of individuality which was a feature of the school in the '60s and '70s, her school career also illustrates the high standard of staff appointed by Miss Ayre and Miss Seward at a time when there was a general shortage of teachers. A high profile in the '80s and '90s means the attention of tabloid newspapers, and Miss Clark and Miss Humphrey would doubtless be shocked by some of the apocryphal stories printed about Belinda, but they would have been thrilled that a Crohamian was in a position to do so much in high places to encourage the Arts, and could still feel that Croham Hurst had 'cherished her individuality and trained her in intelligent habits of thought', in the words of the early advertisements.

Miss Seward's headship was a busy time with many changes. Events which seem to stand out in people's memories were dramatic productions, or foreign trips like the lacrosse team's visits to the U.S.A., or the usual misdemeanours which seemed spectacular to the participants but not significant in the history of the school. The 75th Anniversary was during this time and was marked by showing on the Open Evening records of life 75 years before, the library books popular in 1900, and photos of the old school and former events. The Old Crohamians held a wine and cheese party. This year the 75 Fund was set up, with the governors as trustees, to provide help for parents who found themselves in financial difficulties at a crucial time in their daughter's education. The school grew steadily in size, but was still small enough for each girl to be known by most of the staff, so that discipline could be maintained easily and individual development fostered. Old-girls coming back sometimes regretted the more casual manners and dress, and the more frenetic pace of work, but it was still a place where individuals mattered, where responsibility to the community was emphasised, and where beauty in art, music, dance and literature were appreciated. No great drama like the evacuation to Somerset, or the change to a governing body, or even the headmistress marrying the vice-chairman of the governors, enlivened this part of the school's history. But for each pupil there were highlights of their time there, and ways in which their life after school was influenced. Perhaps the most suitable of Miss Clark's mottoes for this time would be, 'By the street of today, men go to the house of tomorrow'.

CHAPTER 5

Since 1987

'Change is constant'

Those who founded schools in the past were often visionaries. Certainly Theodora Clark was. She was motivated by a vision of what was good and beautiful, and an idea of what skills and subjects needed to be taught and what methods used to hand this vision on to the next generation, and to mould the characters of those who came to her school in accordance with the vision. Different visions had inspired the founders of 16th-century grammar schools, 18th-century 'ragged schools', 19th-century public schools. The vision determined the values inspiring the schools, and also what was taught, and the methods used to teach it. Even when a complete system of state schools was set up, partly because technological advances meant that everyone in the land needed to be literate and numerate, the state still allowed private schools to exist and to experiment. In England, freedom of choice is one of our most firmly held values. This has meant that the British government, although it accredits the teachers, has in the past allowed the content and method of lessons and the choice of subjects taught to be defined largely by the teachers, which means also those who train the teachers and the various boards which set the public examinations. This was, of course, subject to a certain amount of supervision by the Department of Education and Her Majesty's Inspectors. This decentralised decision-making was unlike the system in many other countries.

In the late '80s and '90s, however, the British government became uneasy about what was being taught and how it was being taught. So political intervention increased, not only in the funding of schools and accreditation of teachers, but in the content of lessons and methods to be used. Political changes have to be carried out quickly—before the next election. Consequently in these years there was a continuous flow of new initiatives, without sufficient time to implement them. Independent schools were affected as well as state schools. It would be difficult to find anyone teaching in the late '80s and '90s who did not feel harassed by the number and pressure of directives demanding change—quickly.

Joan Shelmerdine, the new Head of Croham Hurst, had had administrative experience before, as Head of Christ's Church School, Richmond, and previously as Deputy Head of Purley Girls' School for eight years, and Senior Teacher of John Newnham School for two years. She was Croham Hurst's first scientific head, having read Physics and Maths at St Andrew's University, after her school days at Manchester High School

for Girls. She said she was drawn
to Croham Hurst largely because
of its size—a school large enough
to have a wide curriculum but
small enough for each girl to be
significant in the school, and for
the girls to be seen in their family
setting, and to be cared for individually. She did not stand on ceremony, and liked to talk to pupils
individually. Her smile was virtually motherly when at her first
assembly she invited them to come
and enjoy the pictures of her cats
in the drawing room, and the relaxed atmosphere she created was
appreciated. She was glad to accept

81 *Miss Shelmerdine*

the governors' intention that the head should continue the underlying Christian tradition
in the school, and she used Assemblies to talk about her spiritual philosophy. She was
particularly interested in curriculum development, which was certainly going to be
necessary in these years of government changes.

The first challenge was to implement changes brought about by the substitution of
GCSE (General Certificate of Secondary Education) for Ordinary Level School Certificate. This involved much more project work for pupils, which was of course expensive
in time and resources. Most of the text books for examination forms had to be replaced.
Staff had to be trained in new methods of teaching and assessment, as well as in the new
contents of the syllabus. The governors had to find the money to finance the INSET
courses (In Service Training) and 'cluster' meetings to which staff were sent. This particular change went through smoothly, though in some subjects the syllabus was changed
several times. Although the problems were successfully dealt with, a lot of extra work was
created.

The change in the syllabus for GCSE, painful though it seemed at the time, was only
a precursor to the imposition of a National Curriculum in 1989. An independent school
has no choice about following the changes in public examinations, unless it is not going
to present pupils for them. But the National Curriculum was not made compulsory for
schools outside the state system. The governors and head have therefore to make decisions
about how far they can afford to be different from state schools if they deem the
curriculum to be inappropriate for their school. It is a new experience for British schools
to have the content and the methods of assessment in their lessons laid down by a central
authority, for every year-group from the five-year-olds upwards. Miss Clark's understanding of education—to hand on an individual vision of life and values which encourage
the development of a certain kind of character—was no longer sufficient for a head. Now
the head and governors had to have an overview of each subject, an understanding of
where the imposed curriculum was inadequate, a judgement of how much re-equipping

was necessary or affordable, and how much staff re-training was required. It made management and administrative skills as important as a vision.

These decisions were not made easier by the fact that the necessary overview sometimes seemed lacking even in the people who designed the National Curriculum. For instance, it was not clear for a long time whether History was going to be combined with Geography as a dual subject (that is, to have one examination between them for a shortened course in each subject). At one stage, technology was to be a compulsory subject up to the age of 16 and then that was altered. The actual content of various subject curricula was constantly being adjusted. The Maths syllabus underwent major reorganisation three times between 1989 and 1995.

Croham Hurst took the decision that the school had largely to follow the curriculum, since the Key Stage 4, as it was called, would eventually become the syllabus for GCSE. In any case, it was good to make a transfer of schools easy for pupils who might be obliged to move to a different part of the country. The carrying out of this decision involved detailed discussion with the staff about the effect on each subject in each year group. The parents had to be carefully informed about the changes. There had to be a massive re-equipping in books. The proportion of the week's teaching time that went to each subject had to be reconsidered, and so did the balance, to cater properly for differing abilities. As a result, it was felt neccessary to introduce a 44-period week and a nine-period day.

The departments which did decide to follow the National Curriculum had various problems to grapple with. One was the amount of complicated recording and assessment necessary. In Geography for Key Stages 3 and 4 at one time there were 183 different examinable sections. There were five attainment targets. Each of these could be taught and assessed at 10 different levels, and had to be co-ordinated with a separately specified programme of study. Records had to be kept of each pupil's progress in each separate skill as shown in each sub-section of knowledge, though this was later simplified. The same sort of complicated assessment was required at Key Stage 3 in Maths, which the school started in 1989. Each skill had to be tested three times, and an 80 per cent success achieved, or the section had to be repeated. The level reached in each skill by each pupil had to be recorded on a chart roughly every two weeks, and work handed in had not only to be marked right or wrong, but the level of each separate skill had also to be written on the work.

Another problem was that the curriculum previously taught at Croham Hurst was actually wider in most subjects than that prescribed by the National Curriculum, yet the assessment of it, and the requirements for practical investigations, particularly in the science subjects, were exceedingly difficult to carry out. Some of the questions posed and some of the course work set were irritating to cleverer pupils because the answers expected were so obvious as to seem pointless. For instance, in Key Stage 3 in Science, the expected answer to 'Why are windows of buses made of glass?' was 'It is hard and transparent'; and to 'Why does the door of a washing machine have a seal made of rubber?' was 'To seal the water in'. The decision was taken at Croham Hurst to follow Key Stages 1 and 2 in the Limes, but to allow each department in the Senior School latitude to depart from the restrictive curriculum at Key Stage 3. Further changes in the

public examinations are in prospect at the time of writing, so curriculum development
will still be a necessity, as it has been throughout the 20th century.

   For developing the curriculum, it was necessary not simply to change the propor-
tions of time allotted to subjects, but once again to introduce new subjects. The National
Curriculum required the introduction of technology. It would not seem the best use of
resources in a school the size of Croham Hurst, without endowments, to equip and staff
a technology workshop. Indeed one could argue that schools are not the right places to
learn welding or micro-chip manufacture. But Craft, Design and Technology can be
approached through subjects other than resistant materials and electronics. The decision
was taken to include it in what used to be known as Cookery or, later, Home Economics,
and also for a time in Art and Textiles, and to teach it in the last year of the Limes and
in Years 7 and 8. (The school had reluctantly decided to adopt the new classification of
forms used with the National Curriculum in place of the time-hallowed Lower IVths and
Upper Vths, etc.) The essence of technology is problem solving, how to design, and make
and evaluate. So in Food Technology, instead of emphasis on perfection in practical skills
and presentation, the task could be to design a pizza, having understood the principles
of nutrition, and to evaluate what went wrong in the finished product. In Craft Technology, at Year 7 pupils could be presented with a problem like 'How could Jack get water
up the hill for Jill if they lived at the top and the well were at the bottom?', or 'Design
and make a personalised key ring'. The members of the technology club, formed in 1989,
were, as one activity, asked to design and make the frame of a vehicle which could be
powered by elastic bands. State schools were obliged to teach technology up to Key Stage
4, but many of them also found the resistant material component was impossible to fund
and staff, and have had to abandon it. The National Curriculum was slimmed down by
Sir Ron Dearing, but from 1996 Design Technology has again become a core subject,
and the problem of how far the school should follow the directives had to be faced again.

   Another new subject which had to be introduced if the school were to keep abreast
of modern developments was Information Technology. The school had acquired its first
computer, a 'PET', in 1980. Keith Jupp, then head of Maths, described its arrival in the
1980 *Crohamian*:

   Few members of CHS will forget the last Carol Service, especially walking back
   to school in a downpour! When I got back I had a cup of tea and hoped to
   dry out by a radiator. However … I was persuaded to go out in the rain again
   to take possession of the school's microcomputer. My dampened spirits were
   lifted as I carried it into the Small Hall where many staff and guests noticed
   the newcomer and the word quickly got round that 'Our PET has arrived'.

      There is nothing more deflating than to get a new thing and find that you
   cannot get it to work. I plugged it in, switched it on and it gave me the message,
   'Press play on tape 1'. This was impossible because I had neither the cassette
   recorder nor tape 1. I scoured the manual for relevant advice but could not find
   any suggestion which helped. I went home that evening feeling rather annoyed
   with myself and the PET. But a good read of the manual solved the tape 1
   problem and I felt ready to take on the microcomputer the following day.

Once the microcomputer was installed in cupboard 4, my colleagues and I set about writing programs for it. It often takes a long time to write a program so it is essential that the end product will either do a task which would be very lengthy or involved to do without a computer, or a task which will be repeated on many occasions, thus saving many man-hours.

It all sounds very small scale and amateurish by today's standards. At first the computer was used only for mathematical games. In 1983 a computer studies O-level course for the VIth form was started. As more educational programs were produced, more subjects started to make use of the computer. The 1985 magazine mentions a geography program called 'Puddle' illustrating run-off situations following different conditions of rainfall, and a game about surviving an air-crash by following a river from source to mouth to reach civilisation; you get stranded on the beach

82 *Keith Jupp with the PET*

if you take too long travelling downstream, or you can be attacked by wild animals if you choose to camp in the forest—a novel way to learn some Geography. More and more software became available for schools, and it became obvious that computer literacy was a necessary skill for the future. Members of the maths staff with understanding of computer skills were replaced by specialist staff. At first they were part-timers. In 1991 Miss Shelmerdine appointed a full-time member of staff to co-ordinate and teach Information Technology. The number of computers the school possessed had been increasing steadily, but now the governors invested in a new network. At the time of writing there were 15 stations and a network server in the main computer room as well as an information technology room in the Limes and other computers in various subject rooms and in the library. CD-roms have appeared for pupils to use. In 1996 timetabled IT lessons were given to Years 7, 8 and 9 and the Lower VIth. In time this will doubtless seem as quaint as the arrival of the PET now does, as in the computer world change gallops.

Theatre studies was another new subject which appeared in the timetable. Of course, drama had always been included in English lessons at Croham Hurst, and visits to theatres, and the performance of 'Set plays', House plays, School plays, and Drama Club were always an important part of school life. In 1987, however, Miss Shelmerdine appointed to the English department a teacher trained as a drama specialist. The English department was renamed the English and Drama department. Drama was presented as a separate GCSE subject, and in 1993 Theatre Studies was one of the options at A-level. Drama in Years 7, 8 and 9 was now specifically timetabled, instead of being part of English lessons, with the emphasis on methods and techniques of producing and acting as well as on the literary aspects of plays.

Other new subjects introduced at this time were Business Studies, Spanish, Athletics and Fitness Training. Every new subject means further calculations of how much staffing can be afforded, and how far the existing subjects can justifiably be squeezed in resources or timetable time. The introduction of 'Double Award Science' (which means three sciences are studied but two examination papers are set, giving credit for two science subjects) means that to allow for the taking also of three science subjects separately (for those for whom 'Double Award' is insufficient), the timetable tends to become overloaded on the science side. The National Curriculum covered 10 subjects in 1996. Croham Hurst offered 17 at GCSE and 19 at A-level. The entries in the 1940 syllabus books look so simple by comparison. The A-levels offered then and in the early '50s were only English, French, History and Art.

Other changes of these years which owed their impetus mainly to changes imposed by the government were a change in reports, and in staff training and appraisal. As with National Curriculum changes, the directives on these matters were changed several times, and the legal requirement for them was not binding on independent schools. In both cases, Croham Hurst followed, but not slavishly or immediately. When 'Baker Days'—compulsory training days for staff—were introduced, Croham Hurst also had training days. But staff training, and a greatly increased budget for it, had been accepted as a necessity anyway. When the world is changing as fast as it has been in the last quarter of the 20th century, teaching can no longer be the imparting of knowledge gained at college in a subject for which the individual teacher has an enthusiasm. It has become a skill which requires continuous updating. The governors were enthusiastic for a limited system of staff appraisal, co-ordinated, in Miss Shelmerdine's intention, with personal encouragement for staff to develop in different directions, and take on new responsibilities. Job descriptions and clearly defined responsibilities, things which have become usual in the business world, were the 1990s replacement for 'Tray', the informal discussions over coffee after lunch and dinner in the drawing room, which characterised the early days of the Croham Hurst staff. (In the summer of 1994 a Staff Association was formed which provided occasions for informal discussions between Senior School and Limes staff, but only a few times a term, not daily.)

Termly and yearly reports to parents, in the earlier days, used to be a matter for individual members of staff, and at Croham Hurst great emphasis was placed on qualities of character. Now national policy affected reports also. In the brave new world of the late '80s the government talked about compulsory profiling and Records of Achievement for each individual pupil. The National Curriculum at certain stages required a complicated system of assessing the progress in particular skills within a subject for each pupil. In the light of these developments, Croham Hurst experimented with putting all termly reports onto the computer. This did not suit all subjects, some of which do not lend themselves easily to breaking down into specific skills. But the profiles for leavers, with comments on a whole variety of achievements, have continued to be developed. The personal discussion of reports between the form tutor and the pupil, which was part of the government's order, has also continued, in spite of the large amount of time taken by it.

Another government initiative which was looked at seriously was the idea of a co-ordinated curriculum in the lower forms. As an example, the theme of 'island' might be taken, and the work centred round this theme could include Literature, Mathematics, History, Geography and even Science and Home Economics. This is of course frequently done in junior schools. At the senior level, where teachers specialise, the timetabling becomes very complicated. The necessary planning to make sure that each subject could include the right skills and information to provide the proper basis for later examination work was also extremely complicated—so complicated that the government abandoned this idea, but not before much time and ink had been spent. Joan Shelmerdine's interest in curriculum development certainly had plenty of scope for exercise.

The government pressed co-operation with the parents. As this account of Croham Hurst's past has shown, parents were always welcomed at the school. Now parents seemed to become even more interested in the details of what was taught, and so more effort was put into giving information. 1992 saw two Education Forums, to put to the parents the changes that were being made. A twice-termly Newsletter was started. Parents Evenings and Open Evenings were extended, and the Parents' Guild was encouraged. Some parents started helping with sport, like Mr. Ainger with the new sport of trampolining, and Mr. Vickers with swimming.

For prospective parents, the prospectus was once again altered. Miss Humphrey's brochure of 1936 had been on four unillustrated pages, and talked about the situation of the school and its aims. 'Amongst educational aims the formation of character must ever be prominent,' it said. It was rewritten by Miss Wickham, and again under Miss Ayre, this time with a few black and white photos. The prospectus drawn up by Miss Seward and the Education Committee of the governors had four pages of photos, and talked about how 'the school tries to develop each girl's individual gifts, whether these lie in the academic field or in practical or aesthetic spheres'. By 1987, under Miss Shelmerdine, the prospectus had become a large brochure on glossy paper with colour photos on each page, and it was describing a broad based and challenging education 'aiming to draw out the best qualities of each member of its community in a caring and stimulating environment'. The continuity in the school was shown by the cover photo of the stained glass window, and a photograph of girls using the Small Hall juxtaposed with the same view in the 1930s. In 1993 there was yet another brochure, lavishly illustrated in colour, describing 'a happy school, in which we are concerned with the development of the whole person, and the hope that the girls will emerge as well-balanced young women'.

New subjects and new initiatives do of course require new physical resources. Although Miss Shelmerdine's time did not see any major rebuilding, the existing premises were adjusted to accommodate the changes made. The original dining-room, which had been first a form room and then a cloakroom after the 1960s, was now turned into the information technology room. A music practice room in the Vineyard became a home economics preparation room, with the greater emphasis given to this subject and the movement towards Food Technology. The inclusion of theatre studies as an examination subject was marked by the creation of a drama room in one of the garden wing classrooms, all decorated in grey and black to allow for imaginative uses. But the major building expenses at this time were the necessary repairs to a property dating back to the beginning of the century, such as the rebuilding of the retaining wall in Melville Avenue, and the complete re-roofing of the main building.

The administration of the school had to keep up with developments in technology and the enormous increase in paper work involved in all the changes. One of the first acts of Miss Shelmerdine's time was the installation of an up-to-date telephone system. She also arranged for the computerisation of the office. Obviously the office staff had grown as the school had grown. In the early days Miss Ellis had really acted as school secretary with some secretarial support from Miss Jupp and Miss Wilson. When Miss Ellis retired from the school in 1921 Miss Honey combined the secretarial duties with being the Latin teacher. Lilian Murrle also combined secretarial duties with teaching in the junior section under Miss Humphrey. With the change-over to being a charitable trust run by a Council of Governors there had to be a properly appointed Secretary to the governors, a position held by Miss Hardstone and then Miss Mitchell. In 1961 Mrs. Ebison became Bursar and Secretary to the governors, while Mrs. Betty Moore was the headmistress' secretary. When Mrs. Ebison had to retire through ill-health, Wing-Commander Geoffrey Buckland took over the job. His previous experience, 32 years in the Royal Air Force, had included dropping supplies behind the lines in Burma during the war. In the course of his service he had visited 85 different countries. Croham Hurst might seem tame by comparison.

By now, as there were no boarders, and therefore no matron, the job of bursar included appointing and controlling the domestic staff; caretakers, gardeners, maintenance men, caterers. It involved dealing with the fees, both suggesting the levels to the governors and managing the day-to-day financial transactions, for which he had two secretaries to help him. The position of Clerk to the governors, which he also held, was a most important part of the job, and required very different skills from those necessary to decide if the pond needed clearing out or other mundane domestic matters. The headmistress' secretary moved downstairs from the room which had been the head's bedroom in the early days to the area which had been the kitchen before the building of the new Assembly Hall. Wing-Commander Buckland, sitting in his executive's chair in the room that had been Miss Clark's home, never seemed to be in a hurry and never rattled. In spite of the relaxed attitude he created in the office and his old-world courtesy, he spent many hours working out the best way of placing the money on account to bring in the best return. He also had to oversee the large amount of building in Miss Seward's time and the work involved in the Appeal. He retired in 1986 to everyone's regret.

The Wing-Commander's successor was a Navy man, Commander Mundy. He was as keen as Miss Shelmerdine to computerise the administration of the school. The first phase, on which a lot of work was done by the head's secretary and the school secretary, included the use of 'System-Builder' for school records. Of course, in computing, every system becomes out of date very quickly. The Bursar's office, which had expanded to deal with the increased paper work, both in the school administration and in the Bursar's role as Clerk to the governors, now uses a straightforward computerised accounting system.

The head's secretary involved in all this was Gill Chapman, whose cultured tones and competent charm had been most parents' first introduction to the school, as well as many a person's port of call in a storm. She had been the head's secretary since Betty Moore's retirement, so her total service was 22 years. The position of school secretary had been created to cope with the great increase in paper work necessitated by the new methods

83 *The secretaries in the 1980s. Gill Chapman is seated right, Diana Dale standing left.*

84 *Mr. Neale*

of teaching. Barbara Andrews had held this post, but at the time of the computer development it was the ever-obliging and efficient and cheerful Diana Dale.

When Commander Mundy left, a chartered accountant, Mr. Tim Neale, was appointed Bursar and Clerk to the governors. His support of the school, his skill and expertise in finance and law, and knowledge of the business world are much appreciated by the governors, who rely more and more on the clerk and his office in dealing with the increasing paper-work they have to contend with. His suit and tie with matching hand-kerchief might imply that his work was concerned purely with high finance. Like other bursars, he finds that the maintenance of and alterations to the buildings, which have recently included new security systems and fire precautions, absorb much time, as does attention to administrative aspects of school functions, though he doubtless gets more personal satisfaction from the parts of the job which involve dealing with figures. The administration of the school is now very different from Miss Ellis' informal office practice and the painstakingly hand-written account books to be found in the archives!

Administration may be different, but maintenance has not changed much over the years. In the early days, when the school was home to the head, to some of the staff, and to the house-girls, there were of course many servants. For instance, there had to be a man to look after the horse, who had a stable where the present workshop is. In 1922 the gardener Mr. Johns died at the age of 82! Miss Balcombe, in her reminiscences, mentions the next gardener Mr. Beck, who always wanted to talk to her about Gladstone. She also refers to Tilly, the kind-hearted maid who held up the breakfast bell for late-

85 *Mr. Johns*

comers, and Elsie who, when waiting at table on some of Miss Clark's important guests, was heard to whisper 'Have some more of this, it's very good'. Under Miss Humphrey there was of course the be-loved Mabel Waite, and the housekeeper Miss Timewell who, in addition to all her other duties, made vast quantities of marmalade for the house-girls' breakfast. This was more popular than the raw carrot salad for which some people remembered Miss Organ, a later housekeeper. Not all the housekeepers and matrons were loved by the girls. Some house-girls blamed them for hurts such as the disappearance of birthday cakes sent by parents. (When food in-cluded Bemax and porridge for breakfast and bread and dripping for break, a birthday cake was a great event.) There are also memories of what seemed like rather erratic discipline. Bathnight was decided by a finger pointed, apparently at random, as girls ascended the staircase. Talking after lights–out was punished by being made to stand in the Small Hall. A girl was once forgotten till well into the night, as, cold and

86 *The domestic staff in 1920*

87 *Mrs. Justice in 1988*

frightened, she watched the lights from the road light up St Ursula in ghostly fashion. Perhaps it was not easy to find housekeepers and matrons in England at that time. Some of them were foreign, as the names of Miss Klumper, Miss Visser and Mrs. Gamahl testify.

It has never been easy to find caretakers, as it is a job involving long hours and great flexibility. Mr. Rootham was an ex-policeman, and so used to such flexibility. Mr. Marsh was hampered by a trail of children following him wherever he went. Mr. and Mrs. Wright (who left in 1973) and Mr. and Mrs. Trowman made friends with many in the school. Mr. and Mrs. Coldrick, in the senior school from 1980 to 1995, and Mr. Gubby at Limes showed much sympathy and understanding with the pupils and entered into the life of the school with enthusiasm. Mrs. Coldrick was unfailingly good-humoured in a job which was irritatingly diverse, Mr. Coldrick was immensely loyal, and Mr. Gubby was very adaptable. His jobs included rescuing teddies from trees!

Back in 1957 Mr. Shevill was the only maintenance man. He was joined by Mr. Mitchell in 1959. 'Mitch' retired in 1970 at the age of eighty. (Age seemed no bar to the non-teaching staff at Croham Hurst. Mrs. Justice was over seventy before she retired as cook in 1992, having been in the kitchen at Croham Hurst since 1963.) Leslie Talbert, another all-round 'mender' and excellent carpenter, died suddenly and young, but his son Michael stepped into his shoes. Michael not only replaced light bulbs and mended furniture like maintenance men before him, but adjusted to the advancing technology and was able to re-adjust the video recorder and do clever things with computers.

Technological advances and government directives are not the whole story of the late '80s and '90s. Fay Clarke, who had become the first Deputy Head in 1981,

88 *Mrs. Fay Clarke*

89 Oliver

continued daily to arrange rooms and cover, and deal with problems, as the senior mistress had always done, though her unobtrusive style and determination to treat everyone as a responsible adult was her own contribution. She maintained a degree of continuity under three different heads, in particular helping to implement the major changes that took place during this time. Her quiet way has taken the heat out of many difficult situations, and her amiable and friendly attitude has soothed many ruffled feathers.

The other staff continued to teach their forms with enthusiasm and care as they had always done. Some had been there a long time, like Christine King whose calm presence was first seen in Croham Hurst in 1965, though she had spent the years 1968–76 bringing up her children. For much of her time she was co-ordinator of the VIth form, providing advice and personal support to year after year of girls. Doris Payne was another long-serving teacher, always efficient and dedicated and in control and yet somehow self-effacing. The same could be said about Christine Vigurs, the Head of Geography and for much of this time administrator of the examinations, and also of Lesley Pearson who had been in the maths department for many years. One is tempted to talk of a Croham Hurst type, though this would not do justice to the individuality of these long-standing teachers. Others had only been recently appointed, but it was still a group of highly dedicated, caring teachers, many of whom were also inventive and could well have sought promotion elsewhere but chose to stay at Croham Hurst because of its particular atmosphere and strengths.

Music continued to flourish, as it had always done at Croham Hurst. The choir continued to do exciting things, the competence of some of the singers enhanced by the arrival of a visiting singing coach to swell the growing number of peripatetic instrument teachers. Singers from Croham Hurst joined in musicals with Whitgift, including *West Side Story* in 1991. There were three productions at Croham Hurst which involved close collaboration between the music and drama departments; *Oliver* in 1989, *Viva Mexico* in 1992 (with large numbers of enormous Mexican hats), and *Calamity Jane* in 1994. *Barnum*, in 1996, involved not only actors and singers but jugglers, acrobats, clowns, tumblers, dancers and even a uni-cyclist. It was a most elaborate and highly successful production with 100 pupils in the cast. Instrumental concerts continued, gaining a particular professionalism by the quite outstanding piano playing of Mirei Tsuji, one of the school's Japanese pupils. She went on to study piano performance at the Royal Academy of Music. Enthusiasm and enjoyment in making music could be seen on a very wide scale at the 1997 Summer Concert, when performances were given by the Flute Choir, the Jazz Group, the Senior Choir, the Senior Chamber Choir, the Junior Choir, the Junior

90 *Mirei Tsuji*

Chamber Choir, the Senior Orchestra, the Junior Orchestra, the Recorder Group and various soloists. This was also the year in which the choir toured Canada. Pauline Stone, head of music, encouraged this proliferation of opportunities and a very large proportion of the school was fired by her to get excited about music-making, giving up holiday time for practices. Visits to art exhibitions and to dramatic productions also continued in time-honoured fashion.

In Physical Education there was a widening of options. By 1994 girls were encouraged to choose from as many as 23 different sports, including hurdling, basket ball and fencing. It was no innovation to encourage teams to enter for outside competitions, but it was now encouraged even more. In 1991 the trampolining team came third in the National Schools' Trampolining Competition. In 1990, under Mrs. Sally Carmichael, the first gym teacher specially for the Limes, the Juniors came first in the London and Kent region of the British Schools' Gymnastic Association competition.

Innovations during these years included the introduction of a Book Week, and a Writers' Week, when real live writers came to the school to talk to classes and to be questioned, among them Dylan Thomas' daughter Aeronwy Ellis, and Leon Garfield, who allowed Croham Hurst to give the first performance of his next play. An annual general knowledge quiz was organised by Mrs. Pailing, head of Maths. The general knowledge required was wide ranging and not necessarily acquired in school. It was perhaps more likely to be useful for crosswords—questions like 'Who are also known as Canaries, Wolves, and Lions?', or 'What will there always be while there's a country lane?' It could almost fall into the category of an 'occupation'. In the 1940s the school had adopted a ship as a link with the wider world. Now a new link was forged, in taking advantage of Croydon Borough's twinning with Arnhem. It started as pen-friendships with pupils at Lorentz College. By 1995 it extended to a visit by the Deputy Head of the College to Croham Hurst and the visit by Mrs. Redshaw from Croham Hurst to Arnhem. 1993 also saw the first visit, later reciprocated and repeated, to Allen High School, Allentown, USA. Visits to France, which had been organised by the Modern Languages department since the 1950s, were made even more of an integral part of school life by the exchanges during term-time with the College de Jean Baptiste de la Salle.

There were various occasions which affected the whole school, not just some pupils, in these years. The chestnut tree in the middle of Croham Road, about which earlier generations of Crohamians had sung, was replanted by Miss Shelmerdine in November 1988 after the previous one had fallen in the Great Storm. The next year was the 90th birthday of the school, and was celebrated with a soirée somewhat similar to the early

'Exhibitions' and with an enormous cake, big enough for every member to have a piece, eaten in the garden where the early Open Days and Lists were held.

This was the year that the Old Crohamians' Association Benevolent Fund was registered, though the idea, pressed by Sheila Koeze, had first been mooted in 1983. The constitution, arranged to give the trustees independence from the O.C.A. so that charitable status could be obtained, and planned to give maximum flexibility, was finally approved at the 1988 Annual General Meeting of the O.C.A. However, the launching of the Fund with a wine and cheese party and a dinner in the House of Lords took place in the 90th anniversary year.

91 *The planting of the new chestnut tree by Miss Shelmerdine, the headgirl and a girl from Limes*

The raising of money for charity, which had been an activity of the Guild of Help from the earliest days, reached an hilarious pinnacle in 1988 when £1,362.61 was raised on 'Red Nose Day' by activities as crazy as allowing the older girls to hire a younger slave for the day to do menial tasks for them like carrying books and making toast. The best remembered ploy was the kidnapping of the classics teacher, Steve Addis, at Assembly and the threat to release him so that Latin lessons would take place after all unless a ransom of £40 were paid. (The fact that the school joined in this nationwide organised mayhem is a mark of the all pervasive power of television to motivate and set goals. No school can ignore its power.) There were also discos in Miss Shelmerdine's time, to raise money for charity.

These were special occasions. The giving of money to charity was also continued in the time-honoured and quieter ways. Each house sponsored a child in a developing country, contributing to their educational costs, as had been done for many years. The VIth form Christmas Fair, or Coffee Morning, continued to raise money for good causes. (The Christmas Fair had originally been started to raise money for the Building Fund, but had been carried on to raise money for charity. All the heads of Croham Hurst had been eager to encourage the pupils to think of the less privileged.) The VIth form also continued to organise the Christmas party for elderly people which had replaced the parties for 'poor children' in Kennington which were discontinued in 1963. The co-ordinator of much of the charity giving was Wendy Gilbert, whose legendary sense of humour had lightened the school since she joined in 1969, first in the Limes and then as head of Religious Education in the senior school from 1976. By this time R.E. was an A-level subject, no longer called Scripture and taught by the headmistress as it had been under Miss Clark and Miss Humphrey. Mrs. Gilbert's capacity for explaining the theological differences of denominations, or for dealing with misbehaving or unhappy pupils was combined with the ability to write a complete pantomime for the staff to perform to the school in 1983, to tell many an absorbing story in Assembly, and to act the smile of the Cheshire Cat in the staff production of *Alice* in 1979.

In 1992 there was a visit from one of Her Majesty's Inspectors, though this was not a full inspection. He spoke of the girls as charming and responsive, and mentioned the high standards of work on display, and the busy and committed atmosphere. He noted that there was very little spoon-feeding and that girls were encouraged and challenged to think for themselves. These were all features of Croham Hurst from earliest times.

Perhaps the greatest change of this time was the retirement of Miss Meadows from the Limes. She had come to Croham Hurst straight from college in 1949, and had become Head of Limes when Miss Penny retired in 1967. Though she delighted in the whole school, she particularly loved the four- and five-year-olds, and she had special gifts in putting at their ease small girls who came for interview and were too shy to speak. She was even seen down on the floor doing bunny hops at one interview! Generations of Crohamians had been welcomed by her and gently initiated into what was regarded as 'suitable behaviour'. She managed her department by consensus, doing what seemed right after general discussion. Harmony among the staff was maintained by appointing staff who would fit with the existing members. She worked particularly closely with Miss Seward, with whom she saw eye to eye on policy and attitude. Her ways of coping with upset children or over-anxious or over-protective parents were masterly. Her deputy for many years and the highly respected teacher of the Lower IIIrds, Brenda Green, also reached retirement a few years later. There was always a stream of senior school girls coming to the Limes to see Miss Green, and relive their happy times in the more intimate setting of the Limes. It seemed the end of an era when neither Brenda Green nor Peggy Meadows was there.

92 *Brenda Green*

Miss Meadows was replaced by Mrs. Leppington for one year, and then by Sandra Knight, who came to Croham Hurst from Greenacre, a school with similar ethos. Like so many others, she was drawn to Croham Hurst by its friendliness. Of course, government directives had to be taken into consideration in junior schools as elsewhere, and after Miss Meadows' retirement the Limes had all the agonies of accommodation to the national curriculum, and a complete rethink of

93 *Sandra Knight*

94 *Mrs. Carter-Pegg*

the teaching of Mathematics in particular. Mrs. Knight, who continues the Croham Hurst tradition of care for each individual, has also had to think carefully how far National Curriculum and SATS (Standard Assessment Tests) should be followed in the junior section of a school like Croham Hurst. This has been done by careful discussion with staff at every stage, and has involved updating the facilities in the Limes, particularly in Information Technology and Science. It also involved a vast increase in the paperwork, to help with which the Limes now has its own secretary.

It was during Miss Shelmerdine's time that Mrs. Carter-Pegg was elected as Chairman of the governors. On Miss Hinks' resignation in 1984, Mr. Anthony Bradman had become Chairman. He had taken a keen interest in the school where his only daughter Joanne was a pupil, and kept a firm hand on the finances. When he retired from his position as Group Financial Controller of Morgan Grenfell and Co. he went to live in Scotland, where he died in 1997, brave and cheerful to the last as he always had been. Mr. Martin Plater, another father of a pupil, became Chairman for two years. He retired quite suddenly for business reasons in 1993, though he remained a governor. Margaret Carter-Pegg, who became Chairman at this point, had herself been a pupil at the school under Miss Humphrey, and was Miss Wickham's first Head Girl. She became a governor surprisingly young in 1958, and her own daughter and even briefly one of her sons had also been pupils at the school. She was for many years Secretary of the Old Crohamians' Association, and represented it on the Association of Representatives of Old Pupils Societies, becoming the first woman Chairman, and on retirement after nine years also the first woman Vice President of this organisation. In March 1997 she was elected to the Executive Committee of the Governing Bodies of Girls' Schools Association. She has for some years taught English to Japanese girls in the Limes and the senior school. She has lived within sight of the school for most of her married life, and it would be difficult to find someone who knows more about the school or cares more for its welfare.

Miss Shelmerdine did not enjoy good health towards the end of her years at Croham Hurst, and she retired a little early in 1994, to work part-time as a Schools' Inspector with the Independent Schools' Joint Council and with OFSTED. On her retirement the Old

Crohamians gave her a garden party in Mrs. Carter-Pegg's beautiful garden at which they showed their appreciation and presented gifts from the OGA. She was succeeded by Miss Sue Budgen, who came to the school from her post as Deputy Head and Head of English at Surbiton High School. She had also worked at Sutton High School and The Lady Eleanor Holles School at Hampton. She was educated at Godolphin and Latimer School, and at Exeter University, where she obtained an Honours Degree in English. After a spell in the Diplomatic Service, in MI6, she did her training in education at Lady Margaret Hall, Oxford. Miss Budgen, elegantly dressed and soft-spoken, with a love of literature and an incisive way with words, is another head drawn to the school by its family nature, the sense of

95 *Miss Budgen*

community which includes old girls, past staff, governors who are parents or past pupils, and pupils who are in the school because their mothers, aunts and sisters were happy there. (At one stage in the '80s there were eight cousins, relatives of the Wagstaffs who had given the Library, all in the school together.) Like other heads, she has hopes for further developments, particularly in the Sciences and Technology, and in improvements to the buildings. Like all the heads, she cherishes the traditions of the school.

The choosing of the head-girl and deputy head-girl through election by the whole VIth form as well as by the staff, and the role given to them, is one of these traditions. This account, from *The Crohamian* of 1995, could have been a description of the position from any one of the last 30 years, except for the mention of the newly formed VIth-form committee, and the actual appearance of the two girls:

> Watch your thoughts; they become words.
> Watch your words; they become actions.
> Watch your actions; they become habits.
> Watch your habits; they become character.
> Watch your character; it becomes your destiny.
>
> Frank Outlaw

First there is the thought; 'We really are Head Girl and Deputy', then come the words and the actions; speaking at Speech Day, greeting parents at Open

Evening, chairing committees every term. Is it possible that these things can become part of your character? Is it too melodramatic to suggest that reading out 'Merits' and 'Credits' every Friday will have a bearing on your destiny?

After a year in office as Head Girl and Deputy we feel this is an appropriate description of our roles. We were elected to these positions in April of 1994 and to say that it came as a shock would be an understatement. Throughout our time at Croham Hurst the Head Girls and their deputies have always seemed to be so sophisticated and self-confident. It is a fearful moment when you suddenly realise that you are expected to show the same level of maturity. For two girls who claim to have the combined mental age of six this seemed like an impossible task! However, we have come to realise that with the kind of excellent support we have received from staff and the girls in our year the task is not insurmountable.

So what have we been doing all year? Well, as mentioned above, a lot of our time was taken up attending various events, representing the girls of Croham Hurst. This year we had the opportunity to take tea in luxury at the Hyde Park Hotel with the Old Crohamians' Association. We also followed tradition by taking part in Speech Day, the Carol Service and the Sixth Form Forum. In school we have both been heavily involved with various committees such as the Catering Committee, School Council, and the new Sixth Form Committee. We have both learnt a great deal from each of our activities and have enjoyed every aspect, not least the fact that we seem to get fed wherever we go!

However, the main concept we have come to appreciate is that the titles of Head Girl and Deputy are not mere labels to be donned at events like Speech Day. It is probably the only aspect of our positions that you cannot be prepared for. We have both experienced being asked difficult questions, the answers to which we probably don't know. We are still expected to make reasonable suggestions, or at the very least be able to find out what the answers are. On many occasions we have been required to take control of a situation unexpectedly, or come up with contingencies at a moment's notice. Neither of us claims to have been at all successful in these endeavours but we certainly appreciate the value of making an attempt. If nothing else, we have learnt the importance of versatility, diplomacy and humility. We can only hope that we have justified our election to these positions of honour.

The lessons we have learnt as Head Girl and Deputy are the kind that will benefit us long after we have left Croham Hurst. It is for this reason alone that we maintain that our positions have become part of our destiny.

Lia Ali and Lehvashnee Naidoo

Traditions have been kept but some changes have been made. Some are very minor, like the abandonment of the public reading of 'Merits' and 'Credits' in Assembly mentioned by Lia and Lehvashnee. Some are more wide-ranging. Miss Budgen, like Miss Clark, is very aware of appearances. The appearance of the front garden and the Limes grounds immediately caught her eye. Improvements have been made to reception areas and the odd wasted and untidy corners left by previous building changes have been used to provide space for archives, an IT room for staff, and resources for modern languages. New doors and staircases have been added in response to fire regulations. The Limes have had a carefully designed new Library, a well-equipped Science and Technology Room, and an Information Technology Room. The VIth-form accommodation has been refurbished. Other changes are being planned, with facilities for Design and Technology receiving particular attention.

In 1996 the Limes had been part of Croham Hurst for 50 years. The governors, Miss Budgen and Mrs. Knight planned a splendid celebration. Eighty invited guests were shown round the new rooms. Lord Bowness, accompanied by his daughter Caroline who had been a pupil, unveiled a plaque commemorating the occasion. Lunch for these guests was followed by buck's fizz and cake for parents and friends, and blue balloons were released on the field, to float all over Croydon. In the evening there was a disco, which would not have featured in the earlier Jubilee celebrations of the school.

Like other heads, Miss Budgen has planned for curriculum development, adding Spanish and Classical Studies at GCSE, Media Studies GCSE for the VIth form, and French in the Limes from the age of eight, together with developments in Information Technology, Design Technology and Science. To do this it was necessary to introduce a 45-period week. (Oh for those leisurely days of lessons only in the mornings under Miss

96 *The Limes 50th Anniversary. From left to right—Mavis Willifer, Miss Budgen, The Mayor of Croydon, a Limes girl in the uniform of 1949, Caroline Bowness, Lord Bowness, Mrs. Carter-Pegg, David Holloway, and Mrs. Sandra Knight.*

Clark and Miss Humphrey!) Attention is also being paid to computerising the Library, extending careers education and tightening up on educational monitoring procedures and reviews. Marketing now has to be an important part of any head's job, whether in the state or the private sector, and Miss Budgen has paid great attention to singing the praises of the school to parents and press. She has stated as her first aim to raise the expectations of the staff, girls and parents, to encourage initiatives and extend possibilities. As always, it is the intangible but vastly important inspiration which creates confidence that sets a stamp on a school. 'Aiming for a star', Miss Clark would have called it.

In 1996 there was a Quality Management Audit of the school by the Independent Schools' Joint Council in association with Girls' School Association, to which the school belongs. The members of the inspection team enjoyed their three-day visit to Croham Hurst, and observed that 'the school is well managed, and both Senior and Junior Schools function as a very friendly, supportive and orderly community which provides pupils with a sound foundation for the future'.

Miss Budgen's arrival is too near the time of writing for any sort of historical perspective to be possible. But as the centenary of the school's foundation approaches, what is remarkable is how much continuity there is in spite of constant change. Sylvia Bryant, who was a pupil from 1938 to 1942 and on the staff in 1950 and from 1967 to 1972, said at Miss Meadows' retirement party, 'How is it possible for a growing and constantly developing institution like C.H.S. to remain so unchanged in spirit and trad-ition?'. There was a sort of answer given by Miss Ayre in 1965. She said:

> I am personally most interested in any developments that the future may bring— but not at all apprehensive. There are good and bad faults in any system, and it is largely in the hands of each individual school to make the most of the good and the least of the bad. A school is not something static—it is a living organism, and should as such reproduce its cells at least every seven years if it is to stay healthy. But its intrinsic character does not necessarily change at all. The people who work in it, teachers and pupils, OCs and parents—they decide the real character of a school. The spirit of our founders is not something buried and dead; it is alive, though its expression, in present times, must be different.

Miss Clark's way of expressing this thought was indeed different—poetic and obscure:

> Of all life's children, change is the most virile and enterprising ... Change stands at my shoulder. Let him come out that we may look each other in the face. But how is this? Look into the eyes of an old friend.

Miss Budgen chose to start her letter in *The Crohamian* of 1995 with T.S. Eliot's words:

> Time present and time past
> Are both perhaps present in time future,
> And time future contained in time past.

May this glimpse of time present and time past at Croham Hurst help towards our understanding of and our contribution to time future, wherever we spend it.

Finis coronat opus.

Then and Now

Uniform—Then and Now

Miss Clark
A description by Brenda Duncan (1904-9):

> All the big girls wore enormous black bows on top of their hair, done à la Pompadour, and another at the back of their necks, where it was done in a 'door-knocker'—a doubled-up plait. They wore white blouses with high necks surmounted by a 'Toby Frill', and navy blue skirts down to their ankles.

In summer a sailor hat was worn 'with a new school ribbon. The ribbon was hideous! Pale tussore with a vertical blue stripe and blue spots on either side of the stripe.'

For hockey in 1906 girls wore 'a blue cashmere blouse and skirt, with a string-coloured collar and band, a string-coloured and blue tie, brown boots and stockings.'

Games colours were brooches.

By 1913 the hockey club dress could be a blue djibbah (a shapeless tunic similar to the ones worn at Roedean), a string-coloured top and the brown boots and stockings. Tennis clothes were white dress and white stockings. Blouses and blue knickers were worn for gym (or drill as it was called).

In 1919 deportment badges were introduced. They were of tussore silk, with a blue stripe at the lower end. (Later they were changed to a green diamond.)

The school photos of 1917 and 1918 show the seniors wearing summer dress of cotton with wide collars.

The djibbah soon became the school uniform. At first it was worn with a cream yoke, but after 1920 the yoke was of the same colour as the rest of the garment (Croham Hurst blue) with CHS embroidered in the centre, surrounded by cream dots. In winter a cream blouse underneath was allowed. In summer there was a cream border to the sleeves.

Hats were straw panamas in summer, a dark beaver-skin in winter. In 1924 another hat-band—orange, red and brown open-work—was adopted.

In 1922 blazers were introduced, for those who qualified, with CHS on the pocket. Old-girls could wear them, but theirs had to have the dandelion on the pocket.

In 1927, the year of Miss Clark's retirement, blue tammies were allowed instead of hats. School coats were of blue blanket-cloth. There was a summer frock in light blue with a bodice of tussore silk.

Miss Humphrey

In Miss Humphrey's time the uniform was changed to a cornflower-blue dress of serge, which pupils were allowed to make themselves, with long sleeves and a cuff, a gathered waist, and a detachable cream poplin collar. It was not easy to wash. This gradually replaced the djibbah which was phased out from 1946 onwards. The house-girls had special blue cloaks which were made by Mr. Wills, Mabel Sandy's father. Blazers were still worn, and prefects had white cord sewn around the top pocket to indicate their office.

By 1948 there was a special games uniform: blue long shorts and beige short-sleeved Aertex blouse. Grants and Allders were the stockists for uniform. Mabel Waite made the house-girls dresses.

Miss Wickham

Miss Wickham introduced a blue skirt, a Viyella blouse in oatmeal with a tie and a blue jersey. This was easier to wash than the earlier uniform. The school hat was now beige, with a down-turned brim and a blue ribbon. In summer panamas were still worn. A divided skirt was introduced for games, with a beige long-sleeved T-shirt, a V-necked pullover and long socks.

Miss Ayre

Towards the end of Miss Ayre's time, in 1968, the VIth form were allowed to wear any light blue top and any dark blue skirt. Then, in her last year, they were allowed to wear their own choice of clothes. The rest of the school still wore the oatmeal Viyella blouses. The Junior School had stripey ties, while the rest of the school had plain ones. In summer there was a dress in blue with white checks. This could be bought from Allders or Grants, as could the material if mothers wanted to make the dresses themselves. To begin with uniforms had to be bought from Daniel Neal. Then Grants stocked them, and later an approved local dressmaker, Mrs. Chouter, could be used.

Miss Seward

In Miss Seward's time hats finally disappeared. The school council was always proposing changes to the uniform, even suggesting leg-warmers in 1981. Various changes were allowed. Blouses could be blue, navy polos could be worn under them, a pale blue skirt could be worn in summer, socks could be white or beige or blue, tights could be brown, black or navy. The gabardine coat gave way to a blue duffle coat. The suggestions came in thick and fast, but by the time they were accepted the fashion scene had usually changed again, and further requests for changes were made.

Uniform Now

Summer dresses are only seen in the Limes. An anorak has replaced the duffle coat, but is rarely worn. Blue blouses and blue skirts and blazers seem to be the only uniform clothes worn. Games uniform is a white polo-shirt and short games skirt. The Junior school, however, still wear their tunics and pale blue blouses, with check overalls when necessary.

Helping the less fortunate—Then and Now

From the 1910 magazine:

> The Guild of Helpers has been very busy talking and making garments. During Christmas term there were regular meetings, and it was able to send a large supply of clothes to the Croydon Guild of Help … Now the character of the Guild has somewhat changed, many of its members preferring to make their garments at home instead of joining in the fortnightly meeting at CHS.

In 1922 the Guild of Help report said:

> It was decided there should be a regular subscription;
> £5 to the Invalid Children's Aid Association.
> £5 to the Malleson Home for training Young Servants.

The 1958 account in the magazine:

> This year the Guild of Help have adopted Aurelia Niedzwieka, an eleven-year-old Polish girl, who is at present living in a Home for Refugee Children in Derbyshire. Aurelia has no father and her mother is ill in a German isolation camp, which is in a disused aerodrome. Through the Ockenden Venture we send £10 a year towards Aurelia's maintenance. At Christmas and on her birthday, we sent off parcels from various forms in the school.
>
> During the year members of the Upper and Lower Sixth have been visiting the Cranleigh Old People's home on Sunday afternoons to serve tea. One afternoon in the Summer Term we invited the old people to tea at school.
>
> Our regular subscriptions of one guinea included the National Playing Fields Association, the Union of Girls' Schools for Social Service, the People's Dispensary for Sick Animals, the Sunshine Home for Blind Babies, Save the Children Fund, South African Treason Trial Fund, Polio Research, the Society for the Propagation of the Gospel, Medical Missions, Friends of Canterbury Cathedral, Invalid Children's Aid Association and others.
>
> The toys and books brought at the Christmas parties were given to children in the Crosfield Nursery School and the local hospitals. Groceries and gifts of money were sent to the Darby and Joan Club.

1995 Charity Round-up:

> Collections at the Christmas Carol Service amounted to £200 and the money was divided between the Imperial Cancer Research Fund and the Cold Weather Provision for the Homeless in Croydon.
>
> Members of staff helped to set up the emergency Christmas Shelter in the High Street with gifts of bedding, food and toiletries.
>
> The Lower VIth Christmas Fair was well supported and Father Christmas was able to be there in person again this year! Over £450 was raised and donations made to the form's chosen charities—the Cats' Protection League, the Terence Higgins Trust, Shelter and the NSPCC.
>
> 7BR held a Mini Fair and raised £118.77 for Marie Curie Hospice Care by selling home-made cakes, Christmas decorations and books.

9JS held a sponsored dance during the lunch hour and raised £200 for Macmillan Nurses.

8LP was particularly enterprising and organised two sponsored events—a Fast and a Silence. A magnificent £381 was shared between the Blue Peter Well Water Appeal and Children in Need.

Upper VIth visited the Marie Curie Hospice at Caterham and entertained the residents to a concert of instrumental items and carols.

House sponsorships continue, under the auspices of Save the Children Fund. Four young people in the Third World have had their school fees paid and grants made towards uniform and books.

Guild of Help collections last term were sent to Letts House (Hostel for Young Homeless in Croydon) and the Salvation Army. The Christmas Mufti day money was donated to the Benevolent Fund.

Red Nose Day
8LP raised £45
8JC raised £57
9JP raised £45
10DP contributed £3.70

Y11 held a Cake and Toast Sale for Save the Children's 75th Birthday appeal and made £77.

Fees—Then and Now

No records exist of the early fees.

In 1936 the fees were 12 guineas per term for tuition in the senior school, and 48 guineas for boarders.

By 1955 these had gone up to £30 for day girls. Boarders paid an additional £45 for their keep, which seems not to have gone up in the same proportion as the tuition fees over the 20 years.

In 1965 there were no boarders left. The fees were then £78 per term in the senior school. The wages paid were in keeping. For example, Mabel Waite, the matron, was paid £4 per week.

By 1986 the senior school fees were £630 per term, showing the effect of inflation in the intervening years.

In 1996, as inflation continued and the government-imposed changes increased costs, the senior school fees had reached £1,570 per term.

School Trips—Then and Now

Miss Clark took many trips of senior girls and old girls abroad. They went to: Paris (1909), Florence (1912), Venice (1913), Holland (1914), Florence (1922), Verona (1923).

A poem written by Miss Clark from Rome in 1923:

As beneath St. Peter's Dome
Flashes out a pretty fellow

Gaudy red and blue and yellow
Looking very much at home
This must certainly be Rome.

And the mighty names one meets
Capitol and Trajan's Forum
Whilst the trams without decorum
Jingle down the crowded streets
(and the rain comes down in sheets!)

Ghost meets ghost with angry frown—
'Knave at your Renaissance thieving!
Monuments I wept at leaving
Here you came and pulled them down
Using them for your renown!'

I turn from them I confess
For the messages that tireless
Broadcast by a Croydon wireless
Bring me news of CHS
Adding to my happiness.

Here beneath Italian heavens
Great is my content in knowing
All is well and nothing's going
Wrong at sixes and at sevens.
Thank you, VIth and Peggy Evans!

Miss Humphrey was not a great traveller evidently, and it seems that school trips in the 1930s were confined to the VIth form's expedition to Stratford. This may have had something to do with the unsettled nature of Europe at that time. The war then precluded foreign travel, which seems not to have been renewed as a school activity until 1958. In that year six girls joined a course at the Sorbonne to help with advanced level French, and another party of 22 from the Upper and Lower VIths and Upper VIths went to Paris with Miss Klumper for ten days. Five Upper VIth girls also joined a party from Selhurst Grammar School for Girls in an exchange with a German School near Hamburg.

By 1962 a Swiss ski-ing holiday had been added to the annual Stratford trip. There was also a geography expedition to Wales, led by Mrs. Allsopp, which included a 16-mile tramp through a hailstorm, and nights spent in the Youth Hostel at Capel Curig which was so cold that they needed eight blankets each at night.

Now—1996

The Crohamian of 1996 has accounts of:
    The Year 7 visit to Boulogne
    The concert tour of Austria by the choirs

The German exchange, together with Whitgift, to a school near Hamburg

The third exchange with the Allen High School, Pennsylvania, USA, including visits to New York and Washington.

There was also a French exchange, Geography and Biology field trips, and a visit to the Isle of Wight by Year 6, as well as various visits to art galleries, historical sites and theatres in London.

Some Croham Hurst Authors

Theodora Clark

Apart from a chapter in the *History of the Mount School*, published in 1931, most of Miss Clark's writing was for school events, particularly plays for the Exhibition. In 1910 *Some Dreams Come True* was published by George Allen. Here is a quotation from it:

> We must with averted faces
> Unheeded vociferous call;
> Unwearied our measured pace is,
> And steady our light footfall.

In 1927 *The Treasure of Reydonar* was published by Dent.

Genevieve Burnod wrote *My Keeper* which was published by Marshall Pickering. She describes her time at Croham Hurst as a teacher. Here is an extract:

> As soon as I arrived at Croham Hurst School, two days before the boarders were due, in September 1947, I saw how carefully everything had been planned. There was a quietness about the place, and a goodwill, which I liked from the start. All the staff were very friendly towards me and seemed pleased that a young french woman was joining them. The senior girls seemed pleased as well although I must admit that the 'French table' which was set every day at lunchtime for a different group of twelve girls to improve their conversational French didn't thrill them all!

Barbara Batt, who became Barbara Waller, and made her name as a stained glass artist, published her memoirs in 1994. It includes this passage:

> When our fourth child was born, and number five was on the way, I was suddenly pressed into making the Theodora Clark Memorial window for my old school, Croham Hurst. Longing for a bit of release from solid domesticity, I set about turning our small garden room into a studio. My husband, as yet jobless after the war, put glass doors in the end wall, and up went my easels.
>
> There were many difficulties. The toddler had to be taught to mind glass on the floor. Then there was not enough lead to be had just after the war. This problem was solved by finding some old lead pipes in the attic of my brother-in-law, which I was able to get recast. Then there was the question of where to house the finished sections as they got cemented and completed. The only place available in our small thatched cottage was under our old four-poster bed, and there the pile gradually grew.
>
> We hired the Village Hall at Butler's Cross and mounted and lit up the whole window. In those lean times it caused quite a sensation. I remember a wealthy neigh-

bour came galloping up on horseback to the cottage the day after the show closed. 'Where is the famous window?', he inquired. We had to put the lights on once more.

Jane Waller is Barbara Batt's daughter. She has written several books and says she owes her skill partly to the teaching and inspiration of Miss Rowlatt and Miss Glover (Mrs. Rumbelow). For half the year she does ceramics, and writes for the other half.

Blitz and *Women in Wartime, the Role of Women's Magazines 1939-1945* and *Women in Uniform* were co-written with her husband, Michael Vaughan Rees. She has also written social history books, like *Women in Costume*, knitting books, and children's books, including *Below the Green Pond* and *Saving the Dinosaurs*. A quotation from *Saving the Dinosaurs*:

> The crackling twig noise had been made by the first really large animal Peter had seen: a giant woodlouse, but really giant, with wide feelers searching this way and that. The creature's hind legs copied exactly those in front, belting along like the treads of a tank. If there was a boulder in the way, up and over they crawled, rather than take an easier route. Noises from the creature's mouth tumbled out at the same speed as the legs.

Pauline Cockrill worked in museums, the Victoria and Albert Museum and the Museum of Childhood at Bethnal Green. She is now a world authority on old teddy bears and has written several books about them, such as *The Ultimate Teddy Bear Book*, *The Teddy Bear Encyclopedia*, *The Little Book of Bear Care*, *The Little Book of Traditional Bears*, and *The Little Book of Celebrity Bears*. She claims that preparing a history display for the 75th anniversary of Croham Hurst probably decided her to become a museum curator, and the training in English she received at school, as well as the possibility of a wide range of subjects and a wide variety of visits to art galleries and museums gave her 'the opportunity of a very all-round education which allowed me to have the knowledge and the courage to try anything'. She has travelled widely and now lives in Alice Springs.

An extract from *The Ultimate Teddy Bear Book*:

> Before World War I, teddy bears were bear-like, with pointed muzzles, humped backs, and long limbs. They were made of mohair plush in realistic colours, with felt pads on their feet and paws, and boot-button eyes.

Jacynth Hope-Simpson taught at the schoool from 1954 to 1957. She has written several books, including *Who Knows*, *The Gunner's Boy*, and *Save Tarranmoor*!

Theodora Clark Scholarship Report
of a visit to India in 1990 by Sarah Burns

Once I had arrived in Delhi and the sun had risen (I will omit the horrible hours from 2am to 7am when I sat outside the airport literally frozen with fear), I made my way to the Joint Assistance Centre. This was the organisation I was hoping to work for in India. It operated from a rooftop corrugated-iron room. Volunteers lived in a hostel about 20 km away on another rooftop. Being with other volunteers made the whole transition to rooftop and Delhi living much more fun. To me it looked as if we were living in a half-built concrete jungle on the rougher side of town. It is very interesting that when I returned two and a half months later to this same hostel I did not recognise it; what I remembered as poor and scrappy was in fact wealthier than I supposed. In those intervening months my perception of what was rich and poor had been radically altered.

Delhi was very busy, full of careering buses and smog after dusk. Fortunately it was not long before the JAC volunteers travelled to Orissa for a work camp. This was my first Indian train journey, and it was 72 hours long. We travelled 2nd class and so our carriage was open to a constant flow of human traffic—vendors of tea, fruit and hot food, beggars; some blind and old, singing for a few rupees, others little children who would sweep the carriage out and then ask for money. The passengers themselves were in a constant state of flux. Sometimes there would be 20 people in the carriage, at other times perhaps only 7. When a train pulled into a station a clamour instantly arose as people were pushed and pulled off and on. Sometimes it was almost a riot. A train could be a few hours or a whole day late. It seemed as if it swallowed up the hours as we travelled across the continent. Consequently Indians travel with everything they might need, and they were very generous in sharing it all with us. There was a ladies' carriage in Second class and you could always travel First Class, air-conditioned, if you didn't mind missing out on all the fun.

We were travelling to somewhere 60 km south of Bubanesnar, the capital of Orissa, follow-ing the barest of instructions: "Get to K.D. High School and ask for Mr Panda." At the end of our journey we fell out of the bus onto sleeping dogs, into the light thrown up from the lanterns of the tea-stalls. Dhrobor, Mr Panda's right hand man, was there to meet us. He was a three-fingered drummer and general artiste. We walked to the office of International Youth and Disaster Preparedness in the dark with only the stars and fireflies to guide us, singing hymns to light our way in the night.

ORISSA. I stayed for a month in the village of Sanayapally. For the first two weeks we were engaged in construction work. That would take us, at 6 o'clock in the morning, through the village, shovels over our shoulders, baskets on our heads, bidding a morning greeting of "Namascar" to the villagers. They would look at us as if we were really mad. We were helping to fill in the foundation of a building being constructed for disaster relief. When it became too hot we would return to the compound, fetch water from the well, wash ourselves and our clothes. Then as it became dark we would prepare supper; sift through the rice for any rat droppings, chop the garlic and a few potatoes. When it became too dark and the mosquitoes came out we lit a storm lantern and sat inside. We had a primus stove, but large cauldrons of rice had to be cooked on the earth stoves outside, which were actually built into the ground. Days that passed as simply as this focused themselves naturally around water and food, until the functions of drawing water and cooking became almost ritual to us. At the end of the day we would sit down together on the veranda and eat off leaf plates, using only one hand. (This is the custom, but the other hand was also necessary to keep off hungry stray dogs.) Later, when there were more of us, we took turns serving each other. This gave real pleasure in eating together. Our bathroom was outside under the banana trees and had matting for walls. Washing especially was a time for private thought, when the rest of the day was taken up with curious adults and children, many of whom had not seen a white person before. In village life there was really no conception of privacy—everything is shared, as we found out on the festival day of Laxmi, the goddess of wealth and prosperity.

We left the construction work to take part in a camp for disaster relief. (The UN has declared 1990—2000 The International Decade for Disasters.) At least 100 students from all over Orissa (a particularly disaster-prone region) gathered together for a study course. Unfortunately most of the lectures were in Oriya, making it impossible for us to understand. I had only "toro toro" (a little) Hindi at my disposal. However, we grasped the general drift, and learnt much more by talking with fellow students who had experienced natural disasters in their districts. Even in our own village of Sanayapally children's stomachs were markedly swollen with Kwashiorkor (malnutrition) and many people suffered from T.B. This was not regarded as poverty, however, only as living at subsistence-level.

We settled once more into routine, rising at 5am to wash in the well. Then as the sun rose over the dripping grass we would gather for prayers, both Hindu and Christian. Thus by 6 o'clock we were well prepared for the day. Eating together was great fun. We always began with a shout of "aitcha canna" meaning "good food". The highlight of the day, however, was the cultural programme which took place in the evening. The students performed traditional Orissan dances, songs and poetry (all accompanied by Dhrobor, the three-fingered drummer). When it came to our turn, everyone would always call for us to "disco dance". About to begin a Shakespearian recitation, we danced the twist instead (this to no music). Met with shrieks of laughter and shouts of applause, we danced every night and gave up on the Shakespeare. We must have seemed very silly to the Orissans. Compared to us they were very serious.

We had a lot of fun at the end. Sick of rice for breakfast, lunch and supper, sitting on our stomachs like a stone, and chilli burning our mouths raw, another English girl and I proposed to cook an English meal for the IYDP team. The bliss of eating boiled cabbage and mashed potatoes! However, bland food is nauseating to most Indians and we were told that the food was "unpalatable"! When we came to leave I was sad to leave the beautiful watery meadows and distant blue mountains, and also a way of life in which simple things had the power to make you extraordinarily happy.

CALCUTTA. In Calcutta I had the opportunity to visit Mother Theresa's Mission House. This was a haven of peace and tranquility in the midst of a noisy, teeming city. There was such an atmosphere in all her homes; homes for children, the abused, the sick and the dying—an atmosphere that disarms you when you were expecting nothing but horror. I visited one orphanage where all the street boys from Howrah Railway Station are taken for a wash, brush-up and good feed. The place was full of laughing, dancing boys who climbed all over me and put flowers in my hair. I spent the morning trying to mend their clothes—an impossible task, yet this was not the real job in hand. Spending time fixing a torn shirt did not make a great deal of difference to the garment, but it did make the child feel he was worth some-one's time. I also spent some time in an orphanage for younger children, not so robust as these boys. Some of them had been deliberately deformed by their parents, who had hoped to make them more profitable beggars in this way. There were children here who had never been loved, and consequently did not know how to give or receive it. Their plight reminded me of the hymn:

> My song is love unknown,
> My Saviour's love to me,
> Love to the loveless shown that they might lovely be.

Mass poverty and slum dwellings did not seem as tragic as the sight of these frail children. When I looked at the former, I could at least see a few tender, compassionate moments—when a mother hugged a child to her, or a boy laughed to himself, or a woman took meticulous care over washing her hair, or a group of men had a heated discussion. To me, all these moments showed that life was still important to these people and that they had not given up on it. Perhaps this was also something to do with the special atmosphere in Calcutta. It is said to be a city collapsing, but I felt it was much more alive and regenerating.

BOMBAY. There was not the same atmosphere in Bombay. The city is spread over many low-lying hills and marshland. The greyness of mud and the dust of the traffic, these are the colours that remind me of Bombay, except in the evenings when coloured saris would blow out of the doors of rush-hour trains and fly across the face of the setting sun. I once got caught in one of these rush-hour trains, and can compare it only to a rugby scrum (that was in the Ladies' carriage). Bombay is similar to a modern western metropolis in that everybody is concerned with making a living, making a success of it, and rushing about. The population is exploding and even slum accommodation is too expensive for some. (Bombay contains Asia's largest slum.) The chasm between rich and poor is more apparent here than anywhere else. There are some very rich people here. Meanwhile everyone else tries to scrape a living. There is a business in just keeping the streets clean: one child will gather paper scraps, another bits of material, others will rummage through other people's garbage. In this way India is probably one of the most environmentally sound countries in the world—everything is recycled.

In Bombay I had the good fortune to be staying with a social worker and her family. She was completing her PhD thesis on the rehabilitation of battered and abused women through a government-supported Ashram (sheltered accommodation). Finding a place for these women in Indian society is a far more difficult task than it would be in the West, because all rehabilitation has to take place within the strict social framework of the Hindu caste system. An unmarried, low-caste mother may have to go a caste lower to find a husband who accepts her, especially without a dowry. A properly enforced caste system establishes a stable society, where no-one has the ambition to rise above their station in life. The recent Mandal clause, which sought to reserve more government jobs for "scheduled" or lower castes, produced fierce riots from the middle and higher castes, showing how entrenched the caste system still is.

Working on the women's magazine "Manushi" in Delhi helped me to understand these social complexities further, especially in regard to women. Previously, in Orissa, I had noticed the silence of the female students, and the ease with which they were dominated by the boys. Everywhere else I could not help but notice a predominantly male presence in most public places. Women seemed to stay in the house more, and as their husbands seemed to do a lot of chatting and drinking of tea, I assumed that these women were also doing the bulk of the work in caring for the family. Women doing heavy labour on the roads, or breaking rocks to make cement were noticeable, as these are jobs a woman would never do in England. At Manushi I learnt about the discrimination against girl children, beginning at birth where there is a much higher mortality rate for girls than boys, and continuing through childhood. Girl children are less well nourished and looked after than their brothers. They will leave school much earlier, at 11 or 12 years old to look after their younger siblings, and not until they are married do they cease to be a liability to their parents. Even after marriage it is traditional for a recent bride to be victimised by her mother-in-law. Hindu women wishing to be independent have to break free from this cycle at some stage (unless they are fortunate enough to find a liberal husband). Several women I met had refused to marry. One would only marry the man of her choice, and without a dowry.

GUJURAT. Just as I had gone from the Orissan countryside to the city with such excitement, now I longed for peace after Bombay. I travelled northwest to Kutch, a remote, low-lying region of Gujurat that becomes a virtual island during the monsoon. This land was alternately desert and sand, filled respectively with wild asses and flamingoes. I made friends with the archaeological department in Bhuj, the capital of Kutch, and they took me out on their motor-bike to visit the local archaeological sites. We visited the ruins of a Shiv temple, its exotic carvings similar to the famous temples at Khajuraho. Having obtained a permit from the local magistrate, I set out for the village of Dharavira where a Harrapan (or Indus civilisation) site was being excavated. This site is of great importance because it was the largest, and only Harrapan site outside Pakistan. (Lothal, just north of Ahmedabad was only a port, not a town.) Consequently the Archaeological Survey of India was very excited and had veiled everything in secrecy. Indeed, an American archaeologist working in Gujurat had recently been deported, suspected of spying for the CIA.

The city was built around an acropolis and there were massive gateways at each point of the compass. The western gateway was the best preserved. Its huge stone stairs and massive buttresses reminded me of pictures I had seen of the excavations at Troy. All this was in the middle of the desert, 60 km south of the Pakistani border. During my stay here I lived with the postman (Subnudan) and his family. Their kitchen was partially collapsed and we would cook and eat looking up to the stars. At night the wind was so strong and the stars so fiery in the desert. No one spoke English in this village, yet I took away with me the strongest impression of warmth and love that I had experienced so far.

After this I embarked on a lenghty bus-ride across the desert. It was bitterly cold, there being no glass in the windows. Most of the passengers were huddled up on the floor since the seats would fly off at every bump. The bus would often plunge off the road, in search of some remote desert hamlet, or just to avoid an on-coming camel. I remember these bus-rides as great fun. Sometimes, if there was Hindi film music blaring from the radio it was even better. How different from the single voice of the Messim, calling good Moslems to prayer.

While travelling in India these sounds and smells wove themselves into one rich and colourful tapestry; the cows, the street-vendors singing their wares, the markets, the beggars, the be-turbanned and blanketed men, the traffic chaos, the constant clamour, the huge steam locomotives, the food, the spices, the rubbish, the smell of incense and the sweeter smell of jasmine flowers, ritual cleaning, spitting, squat toilets or communally sharing your toilet in a field, not eating with your left hand, the mosquitoes, the heat, the crowds, the cold in the desert and mountains, the smog in the cities, and howling stray dogs in sticky nights.

I would like to thank the Old Crohamians Association for making this trip possible for me.

CHRONOLOGY

1899	Miss Kathleen Ellis started a small school in Croham Road.
1901	Miss Theodora Clark joined her.
1905	The school building in Croham Road begun.
1909	The Old Crohamians' Association founded.
1910	The first edition of *The Crohamian*.
1911	The Domestic School built.
1914	The Studio added.
1918	'Flu epidemic. The school closed for a while.
1921	Miss Ellis retired.
1924	The Annexe built and the Bungalow in Pilgrims Way acquired.
1927	Miss Clark retired. Miss Berta Humphrey became Head.
1930	The Tower House bought.
1937	Typhoid outbreak.
1938	Bridge House in Somerset rented. Temporary evacuation of part of the School.
1939	Whole School moved to Bridge House in September.
1940	Miss Clark died.
1942	Miss Ross re-opened Tower House.
1945	School returned to Croham Road.
1946	Limes bought and Tower House sold.
1948	Memorial Window to Miss Clark.
1949	Jubilee. Founders' Day service begun.
1951	Miss Humphrey retired. School made a Charitable Trust with governors under chairmanship of Mr. James Patterson. Miss Ross Principal.
1952	Miss Ross retired. Miss Stella Wickham became Head.
1953	Introduction of Houses and end of Form Books.
1955	New form rooms built on ground floor.
1956	Wagstaff Library donated.
1957	Vineyard bought.
1958	Coat of Arms donated.

1959	Diamond Jubilee. Miss Wickham (Mrs. Chamberlain) retired. Miss Molly Ayre became Head.
1961	End of boarding. Temporary Gym erected.
1964	New class-rooms built on top corridor.
1965	Assembly Hall and Kitchens built.
1966	Mr. Norman Freeman became Chairman of governors.
1967	Retirement of Miss Ann Penny from Limes.
1968	Mrs. Bywater (Miss Humphrey) died.
1969	New Laboratories in science block opened.
1970	Miss Ayre retired. Miss Doreen Seward became Head.
1973	Garden Wing classrooms and workshop built.
1974	75th Anniversary. Bywater VIth-form Library. Mr. Freeman retired as Chairman of governors.
1976	Parents' Guild was started.
1977	Jubilee Wing added to science block.
1978	Mr. Derek Rodgers retired as Chairman of governors.
1980	Careers Library in memory of Miss Balcombe.
1981	Limes Gym and class-room built.
1983	Mrs. Chamberlain (Miss Wickham) died.
1985	Doreen Seward Centre opened. Miss Ellinor Hinks retired as Chairman of governors.
1986	Miss Seward retired. Miss Joan Shelmerdine became Head.
1989	90th anniversary. Old Crohamians started Benevolent Fund.
1990	Retirement of Miss Meadows from Limes.
1991	Mr. Anthony Bradman retired as Chairman of governors.
1993	Mr. Martin Plater retired and Mrs. Margaret Carter-Pegg became Chairman of governors.
1994	Miss Shelmerdine retired. Miss Budgen became Head.
1996	Limes 50th anniversary celebrated.
1997	Miss Ayre died.

List of Subscribers

NAME, (MAIDEN NAME), dates at school, status if not current pupil or old-girl.

Alexandra ABSON (GLOVER-MARSHALL)	1929 – 1939	
Joe D ADAMS		Governor
Dr Karen O AKINSANYA	1979 – 1986	
Professor J A AKINSANYA		Parent
Dr Simone ALI	1981 – 1988	
Lisa ALLEN (STAFFORD-HILL)	1979 – 1986	
Jodi ALLEN	1993 –	
Rachel M ALLIN	1982 – 1990	
Zeena AMIN	1994 –	
Fiona ANDERSON	1973 – 1986	
Sheena ANDERSON	1976 – 1990	
Kate APPLEBEE	1979 – 1990	
Nicole APPLEBEE	1980 – 1992	
Sophie ARNOLD		Parent
V T ASHTON	1983 – 1989	
The ATHERTON Family	1998 –	
Rachel Louise AVERY	1988 –	
Margaret J BAKER	1980 – 1990	Governor
Kasia BANNON	1987 –	
Jessica BARTHAUD	1997 –	
Joanna BARTON	1979 – 1990	
Katie J BARTON	1994 –	
Angela BARWELL		Staff
Ruth BAVINGTON (FINNEY)	1946 – 1954	
Barbara P BECKETT	1966 – 1982	Staff
Caroline BEETON	1976 – 1990	
Emma BELL	1993 –	
Francesca BELLOMETTI	1992 –	
Catherine BENSTEAD (SYMONDS)	1947 – 1960	
Mrs. W BEVAN		Staff
Dr J BLAKE		Parent
Megan Nicole BOWER	1998 –	
Kim BOWTHORPE	1977 – 1992	
Joanne BRADMAN	1974 – 1987	
Sophie BRADSHAW	1988 – 1997	
Deborah BRENT (MORRIS)	1957 – 1970	also Governor & Parent
Nicola BROOKBANK	1995 –	
Carol BROOKE	1979 – 1993	

Amy BROOKER	1990 - 1997	
Clare BRUNDLE	1980 - 1994	
Katherine BRUNDLE	1983 - 1997	
Sylvia BRYANT	1950 & 1967 - 1972; 1938 - 1942	Staff and pupil
Miss S C BUDGEN	1994 -	Head
Francesca BURGOYNE	1993 - 1998	
Sophie Anne Louise BURMAN	1989 -	
Georgina BURROWS	1992 -	
Laura BUTTERWORTH	1986 - 1991	
Sarah BUTTERWORTH	1992 -	
Emma BUTTERWORTH	1995 -	
Kay CALDERWOOD	1994 -	
Philippa CALLER (GAGE)	1974 - 1983	
Julia CAMPBELL	1987 - 1994	
Fenella CARDWELL	1960 - 1970	
Kelly CARTER	1987 -	
Christopher N CARTER-PEGG	1977 - 1978	Old Boy
Hallam CARTER-PEGG		Former Parent
Margaret E CARTER-PEGG (MANT)	1946 - 1953; also Former Parent & Chairman of Governors 1993-	
Nicholas H CARTER-PEGG		
Joanna CASEY	1981 - 1990	
Jean CHALMERS (CROOK)	1947 - 1954	
Mary CHALMERS (ALLAN)	1944 - 1957	
Heather Jane CHAPMAN	1992 -	
Tracey R CHEALL (CHUNG)	1975 - 1980	
Ayumi CHIKARAISHI	1996 -	
Mollie CHRISTOPHER	1934 - 1941	
Valerie CHUTER (BORRIE)	1948 - 1956	
Mrs C CLARK		Parent
Alison CLAYDON	1975 - 1987	
Fiona CLAYDON	1981 - 1992	
Hannah CLEMENS	1997 -	
Councillor R W COATMAN MBE JP		Parent
Philippa Mary COBB (PICKERING)	1975 - 1987	
Gordon & Majorie COLDRICK	1980 - 1995	Staff
Georgina COLLINS	1988 - 1995	
Suzanne COLLINS	1985 - 1992	
Sofie COMPORT	1995 -	
Aimee Jane COMPTON	1997 -	
Mary COOKMAN	1927 - 1934	
Caroline COOPER	1990 - 1997	
Ariana COULTHURST	1995 -	
Ros COX		Parent
Susan CRAMERI (EVANS)	1952 - 1956	
Sarah CRANE	1969 - 1982	
Penny CREER (BETTS)	1956 - 1964	
Susan Darwina CROCKER (CLAYTON)	1962 - 1975	
Sheila CROWLEY (BAIRD)	1949 - 1961	Parent
Elisabeth DAILEY	1969 - 1982	
Emma C DALMAN	1996 -	
Natalie DANIEL	1996 -	

Nicola Jane DAVEY	1997 –	
Philippa DAVIS	1974 – 1988	
Julia DAVIS	1989 – 1994	
Natalie DAVIS	1991 –	
Sarah DAVIS	1991 –	
Helen C DEAN	1994 –	
Susan Jane DEAN (HUNT)	1947 – 1959	
D A de MORAES		Governor & Parent
Sophie de SOUZA	1993 –	
Zoe DICKER	1980 – 1994	
Letitia DICKINSON (REID SMITH)	1963 – 1969	
Avril DICKMAN (MILSOM)	1945 – 1962	
Mrs J DRAFFAN		Staff
Barbara Ann DRAKE (FOAT)	1946 – 1956	
Hugh DUNCAN		Governor
Brenda EARNEY (NEX)	1939 – 1950	
Kathryn EBDON	1994 –	
Mrs Evelyn EBISON	1958 – 1973	Bursar
Katie ELDRIDGE	1990 –	
Elizabeth EMSON (IRELAND)	1950 – 1959	
Rina ENDO	1995 –	
Elizabeth FALK	1918 – 1928	
Rosanna FARRAR	1990 –	
Clare Amanda FITZGERALD	1986 –	
Leonie R FLOWERDAY	1988 – 1993	
Catriona FORREST (BOULTON)	1965 – 1973	
Mrs G FOSTER		Staff
Amy Rebecca FOSTER-GOSS	1998 –	
Wendy FOWLER (FORSTER)	1947 – 1951	
Penelope J FOX (WILLEY)	1963 – 1971	
Charlene FRANCOIS (SINCLAIR)	1973 – 1976	
Sir Campbell FRASER		Former Governor
Alison FRASER	1967 – 1980	
Holly Emily FREEMAN	1981 – 1995	
Nicola FRENCH	1988 –	
Miyu FUJII	1993 – 1998	
Yuka FUJII	1993 – 1998	
Cory FULLER	1977 – 1991	
Mrs Sue FULLERTON (NEWBATT)		Staff & Pupil
Catherine FURNER	1985 – 1992	
Alan FUTTER		Parent
Eileen GAGE (MANCHESTER)	1946 – 1951	
Emma GARDNER	1979 – 1993	
Katherine GARDNER	1983 – 1993	
Judith GARLAND (LEYLAND)	1946 – 1955	
Tracey GARRATTY	1983 – 1996	
Laura GENTLE	1989 –	
Jane GIBBON	1986 – 1997	
Katie GIBBON	1989 –	
Diana GILBERT	1993 – 1996	Staff
Wendy GILBERT	1967 –	Staff

Louise GILLARD	1995 – 1997	
Mrs M A GLASS		Staff
Margaret GODFREY	1962 – 1964 & 1974 – 1989	Staff
Morag GOLESWORTHY (MCLEOD)	1947 – 1955	
Justine GOLESWORTHY	1975 – 1984	
Janet GOODWIN (BROWN)	1960 – 1974	
Maureen GOODWIN (ELPHICK)	1967 – 1991	Staff
Susan GOODWIN (PETHERWICK)	1987 – 1998	Staff
Rebecca GORD	1987 –	
Hannah GRAHAM	1980 – 1994	
Anni GREEN	1992 – 1996	Staff
Brenda GREEN	1957 – 1995	Staff
Amy GRIGGS	1983 – 1997	
Bretta Gabrielle GROCER (THOMAS)	1974 – 1981	
Juliette HABOUBI (WINSER)	1978 – 1986	
Cassandra HAGGIS	1986 – 1995	
Katherine HAGGIS	1986 – 1997	
Anne HALL (RUFFHEAD)	1946 – 1955	
Jennifer & Susan HALL	1969 – 1983 & 1971 – 1985	
Penny HALL (DIX)	1964 – 1970	Parent & pupil
The HAMILTON Family		Parent & Pupil
Eleanor HANSFORD	1983 – 1997	
Laura HANSFORD	1985 –	
Sarah HARLOW (HARVEY)	1975 – 1989	
Sophie HARRIS	1997 –	
Colin A HART		Governor & Parent
Delia A HART		Parent
Katie E HART	1981 – 1995	
Jane HART	1962 – 1976	
Dawn-Anna HARVEY	1991 – 1998	
Rosemary Ruth HAYNE	1944 – 1952	
Joyce HENDERSON (FRAYLING)	1949 – 1960	
Janet HERBERTSON (DUDSON)	1946 – 1957	
Vicky HEWETT (CUNNINGHAM)	1970 – 1979	
Diana HEWETT-HICKS (TRUETT)	1945 – 1957	
Mary HEWETT-HICKS	1977 – 1991	
Janet HIBBERT (CUNNINGHAM)	1921 – 1928	
Christina HICKMAN	1997 –	
Ellinor M HINKS	1924 – 1930	also Former Chairman of Governors
Rachel HIRD	1984 – 1997	
Christina HODD (GILBERT)	1942 – 1948	
May HOLLOWAY	1997 –	
Zoe Louise HOLLOWAY	1995 –	
Andree Welstead HORNBY (WELSTEAD)	1945 – 1954	
Jane HOWARD (RIDLEY)	1963 – 1974	
Thelma HUBER (MACKAY)	1953 – 1958	
Kanae ICHIKAWA	1996 – 1998	
Sheila INGRAM		Staff
Hitomi INUJIMA	1996 –	
Margaret IRVINE	1988 –	Staff & Parent
Keira JACKSON	1985 – 1992	

Anna JAMES	1985 -	
Lucy JESSOP	1990 - 1995	
Helen JEYNES	1991 - 1996	
Ruth JOHNSON (WHITMORE)	1986 - 1990	Staff
Suzanne Abigail Kylie JONES	1990 -	
Suzanne Powers JONES	1996 -	
Jenny JONES (TOPPLE)	1963 - 1971	
Kathleen JONES	1957 - 1962	Staff
Keith JUPP	1974 - 1985	Staff
Suzanne JUPP	1978 - 1992	
Yuki KAMINAGA	1997 -	
Rekha KAPIL	1997 -	
Mariko KATO	1991 -	
Yuriko KATO	1992 -	
Jessica Frances KELLEY	1989 -	
Lucy KENNEDY	1978 - 1991	
Rebecca KENSINGTON	1997 -	
Natasha KENSINGTON	1999 -	
John KIDD		Governor
L & J KNIGHT	- 1994	
Jessica KNIGHTS	1994 -	
Chie KOGURE	1998 -	
Susan KOMMER	1979 - 1988	
Sanae KONNO	1976 - 1980	
Sophie KREKIS	1991 -	
Nathalie KREKIS	1991 -	
Katie Louise KYRITSIS	1996 -	
Antonia LANCE	1982 - 1996	
Janine LANDYMORE	1993 -	
G Mary LE FLEMING (CARR)	1920 - 1970	Staff & Pupil
Dominique LE HUR	1994 -	
Shirley LENNON	1997 -	
Sarah LEVERIDGE (HEWETT-HICKS)	1974 - 1982	
Peter LONGFIELD		Governor & Parent
Gordon LUCAS		Husband of Staff
Amanda LYNCH	1990 - 1995	
Joan S LYONS (APLIN)	1927 - 1936	Parent & Pupil
Christina Jane McCARTHY (UNDERWOOD)	1977 - 1989	
Danielle McGOVERN	1998 -	
Ann McKINLAY	1991 -	Staff
Clare MacKINNON	1991 -	
Kuldip MANGLA (DHALIWAL)	1963 - 1969	
Molly MANT		Former Parent
Mrs R C MARSH		Researcher, Whitworth Art Gallery, Manchester
Ayaka MARUYAMA	1997 -	
Shizuka MARUYAMA	1997 -	
Charlotte MASTERS	1987 -	
Ruth MATTHEW	1989 - 1996	
Margery MELLOR	1954 - 1981	Staff
M S G MICHAEL		Parent
Mary MICKLEWRIGHT	1922 - 1931	

Sarah Jane MILLS	1982 - 1992	
Katherine Helen MONIZ	1997 -	
Jennifer Anne MOORE	1946 - 1957	
Lehvashnee NAIDOO	1988 - 1995	
Gael NASH (ROY)	1952 - 1960	
T P G NEALE	1990 -	Bursar
Jennifer NEUBERT	1995 -	
Tamsin Oriel NEWLANDS	1997 -	
Emily Jane NEWMAN	1985 -	
Carole J NICHOLSON (DODD)	1965 - 1975	
Katherine NIMMO (KERSWILL)	1945 - 1950	
Rosemary NORRIS (LONGFIELD)	1965 - 1979	
Rebecca O'CALLAGHAN	1995 -	
Katy OGG	1984 - 1998	
Makiko OKANO	1990 - 1992	
Mrs A L O'REGAN		Staff
Melanie ORME	1972 - 1979	
Karen M OWEN (CARTER-PEGG)	1971 - 1985	
Haley OXENHAM	1987 - 1994	
Susan PAINTER (PELLING)	1954 - 1965	
Lara Joy PARKINSON	1996 -	
Francesca PASSEY	1994 -	
Lindsay PATACCHIOLA (KENT)	1990 -	Staff
Jillian Elizabeth PAYE (SALTER)	1966 - 1971	
Sue PEACOCK (MURPHY)	1952 - 1965	
Lucy PEARCE	1989 - 1997	
Lesley PEARSON		Staff
Mrs S PEATE		Staff
Sara PENNELLS (LING)	1958 - 1965	
Kay PENNY	1945 - 1974	Staff
The PERKINS Family	1979 - 1993	
Sarah PERRIN (CROSBY)	1975 - 1982	
Chris PERROTT		Staff
Susan L PHILLIPS (TURNER)	1960 - 1972	
Sally PIKE (ROBINSON)	1961 - 1971	
Francesca PITTS	1998 -	
Martin D PLATER		Governor
Jennifer PLATT	1994 -	
Laura PLATT	1994 -	
Katherine PLATT	1989 -	
Mrs M PLUMSTEAD	1947 - 1973	Staff
Sue POLLOCK (CONNORTON)	1966 - 1977	
Anne POMEROY	1993 -	
Jennifer POOLE	1992 -	
Eileen POORE	1990 -	Staff
Heidi J PORTER	1974 - 1986	
Alison M J POWER	1987 - 1994	
Crystal Jean PRATT	1987 -	
Frances M PRESS (WALLER)	1953 - 1961	also Parent & Staff
Di PRITCHARD (KENNAWAY)	1959 - 1966	
Sandi PROCTER	1975 - 1979	Staff

Diana RAINE	1994 -	Governor
Elizabeth RAMSAY	1965 - 1976	
Suzanne C RANDALL	1986 - 1993	
Charlotte REDPATH	1983 - 1996	
Mrs E N REDSHAW	1984 - 1995	Staff
Mary RICE (GRIFFIN)	1929 - 1940	
Fiona RICHARDSON	1991 - 1998	
Lucy RIDLEY	1998 -	
The RITCHIE Family	1994 -	
Heather P ROBERTS (WADDINGTON)	1950 - 1960	
Margaret H ROBERTS	1946 - 1951	Staff
Michelle Ann ROBERTS	1997 -	
Francoise ROBERTSON (HERZBERG)	1947 - 1957	
Kirsten ROBINSON	1983 - 1990	
Beatrice (Betty) ROGERS (MARILLIER)	1908 - 1916	
Gillian ROGERS	1947 - 1960	
Hannah ROGERS	1984 - 1992	
Martine ROSE	1988 - 1998	
Elizabeth ROSS (MITCHELL)	1957 - 1970	
Catherine ROURKE	1989 - 1996	
Ann ROUTLEDGE	1976 - 1991	
Jennifer ROUTLEDGE	1988 -	
Annabel ROUTLEDGE	1991 -	
Linda ROWE (BEAUCHAMP)	1972 - 1978	Parent & Pupil
Nicola ROWE	1991 -	
Fiona ROWE	1998 -	
Dione ROWLATT	1945 - 1947 & 1959 - 1982	Staff
Nadia RYMAN	1983 - 1997	
Bill RYMER		solicitor
Helena Mabel SANDY (WILLS)	1926 - 1929	also Staff & Parent
Emma SAUNDERS	1983 - 1997	
Elizabeth SCOTT (ROSE)	1935 - 1943	
Sorrel SCOTT	1980 - 1988	
Patricia SCOWEN (MADDEN)	1948 - 1958	
Kate SEPKES	1984 - 1996	
Victoria SEPKES	1981 - 1995	
Suchita SHAH	1984 - 1997	
Sara SHAWWA	1990 - 1996	
Rosemary SHEARS (KING)	1947 - 1957	
Joan M SHELMERDINE	1986 - 1994	Head
Miyuki & Sayuri SHINOHARA	1995 -	
Joy SHIROI (SAYER)	1930 - 1939	
Caro SIMPER (SHAW)	1962 - 1970	
Fiona SIMPSON (CRAIG)	1967 - 1982	
Laura SIMSON (LOVESTONE)	1974 - 1980	
Daniella SINES	1997 -	
Margaret SKIDMORE (SULLEY)	1946 - 1956	
Carol SMEETH	1985 - 1998	Staff
Elizabeth J SMITH (TOPLEY)	1973 - 1975	
Emily Jane SMITH	1986 - 1993	
Scarlett A SMITH	1997 -	

Gill SMITH	1990 –	Staff
Judy SMITH	1987 –	Staff
Kyla Stevie SMITH	1996 –	
Mrs Sheila SMITH	1986 – 1990	Staff
Mala K SONI	1971 – 1975	
Eiko SONOBE	1995 – 1998	
Hayley SOUTHERN	1997 –	
Lauren SPRING (MURPHY)	1984 – 1991	
Samantha Alexis Marguerite SPRY	1989 –	
Alexandra STYLIANOU	1998 –	
Anne I SYMONS		Parent
Samantha K SZILAGYI	1988 –	
Deborah A SZILAGYI	1979 – 1994	
Jane Muriel TARVER (KESTIN)	1964 – 1971	
Helen TATHAM	1988 – 1995	
Diana F TAYLOR (WOOLLEY)	1948 – 1957	
Christine TAYLOR	1976 – 1983	Staff
Alexandra THIRTLE	1982 – 1996	
Caroline Maxine THOMAS	1985 – 1990	
Lynne THOMAS	1989 – 1994	
Francesca A V THOMAS-HOFFMAN (THOMAS)	1973 – 1981	
Frances THOMPSON	1985 –	
Hannah THOMPSON	1987 –	
Jean THORPE (RIESCO)	1920 – 1929	
Rachel TIMMS	1993 –	
Shirin TIRVENGADUM	1978 – 1982	
Ann TOMSETT	1960 – 1966	
Claire TOOMEY	1996 –	
Vanessa TOPP	1988 –	
Katie TRIBE (SMITHER)	1973 – 1988	
Judy TRINGHAM	1962 – 1968	
Emma TRUETT	1982 – 1989	
Victoria TRUETT	1985 – 1992	
Michael TURNER		Governor
Brian UDELL		Parent
Sheila ULLMAN (BENSON)	1952 – 1962	
Susan C UNDERWOOD	1975 – 1986	
Rebecca UPSON	1997 –	
Anjali VADGAMA	1996 –	
Ketishia VAUGHAN	1990 –	
Gayle J VICKERS	1990 – 1997	
Sue VIGOR	1982 – 1987	
Christine VIGURS		Staff
Mrs Y M VINALL	1985 – 1993	Staff
Nikki WAGSTAFF	1951 – 1959	
Christine WALES (GALER)	1953 – 1962	
Gillian WALKER (BENNETT)	1956 – 1969	
Margaret R WALKER (PAYNE)	1926 – 1937	also Parent
Ruth WALKER (ALLEN)	1918 – 1924	
Josephine WANFORD (LAWTON)	1945 – 1951	
Gillian WARREN (BAALHAM)	1947 – 1949	

Jane Rose WARREN   1990 -
Emma L S WATERHOUSE   1972 - 1987
Helen WATERMAN   1988 - 1995
Rosalind WATKINSON   Parent & Staff & Pupil
Holly WATSON-STEWARD   1985 - 1993
Jacqueline WEBB   1983 - 1997
Mabel WEISS   1920 & 1925 - 1930
Annabel & Cressida WELLS   1972 - 1984
Brenda WHEELER   Parent & Staff
Emma WHITAKER   1970 - 1983
Margaret WHITTAKER (DICKINS)   1932 - 1939
Deborah WILCOCK (GILBERT)   1970 - 1980   also Parent
Elizabeth A WILDE   1991 - 1996
Mavis WILLIFER (HOWELL)   1946 - 1958
Dominique Anneliese WINDMILL   1993 -
Helen WINSER   1978 - 1992
Katherine WINSER   1977 - 1987
Dr Sonia WINSOR (FIELD)   1963 - 1975
Ruth J R WINTER   1976 - 1985
Alison M WOOD   1971 - 1976
Carol J WOOTON   1969 - 1972
Mariko YAMAMOTO   1984 - 1986
Shirley YOUNGWALL (MEREDITH)   1949 - 1957
Christine ZOLLER   1982 - 1992
Independent Schools Council
National Westminster Bank plc

INDEX

Page numbers in **bold** refer to illustrations.